First published 2026

by Starting Where You Are Press

Aotearoa New Zealand

ISBN 978-1-0671327-0-5 (paperback)

ISBN 978-1-0671327-1-2 (ebook)

Printed in New Zealand

YOUR JOB IS A CLIMATE JOB

We don't need a world full of sustainability managers.
We need a world where *everyone*, in whatever role they hold,
chooses to act.

Every job has an impact. Every career has a climate story.
Whatever your title — engineer, teacher, apprentice, director,
installer, analyst, barista — *you already have a platform to
make change*.

You don't need to change your job to do something meaningful.
You need to choose to start.

– Sincerely, a sustainability manager

To Mum, Abigail and Louise - and to Judith,
Thank you for everything: your love, guidance, support, good humour, and your patience (for tolerating years of dinner table conversations about air conditioning).

And to Arya, Elif, Oliver and Áurea,
For the future you each deserve.

Contents

4

Introduction

The writing has been on the wall for years.
The evidence is clear.

Crops are failing.
Wildfires are breaking out around the world.
Sea levels are rising.
Communities are being destroyed by flooding.

The climate is changing.

And. It's. All. Your. Fault.

Or at least, that's what the big fossil fuel companies, and parts of the mainstream media, would have you believe.

In reality?

Just 100 companies are linked to more than 70% of global industrial greenhouse gas emissions since 1988, the year we finally, officially recognised human-induced climate change.

We currently share this small planet with around 8 billion people. By 2030, that number is projected to reach 8.5 billion, and by 2050, 9.7 billion.

The average person's carbon footprint is roughly 4.7 tonnes of CO_2e per year[1]. But that headline number hides staggering inequality. Some people emit more than 50 tonnes annually. Others almost none.

---

[1] Our World in Data, CO2 emissions, 2024.

A recent Oxfam analysis shows that a single person from the richest 0.1% produces more carbon pollution in a single day than someone in the poorest 50% produces in an entire year.

Understanding your own carbon footprint matters.
But it matters even more when you understand how your actions sit inside bigger systems, and how change actually happens.

This isn't a book packed with "life hacks" on how to *live more sustainably*. There are plenty of those already. Some helpful. Some... less so.

For years, we've been bombarded with advice:

"Recycle and all will be well."
"Turn off the lights to save the planet and your wallet."
"Buy an electric car."
"Only wash at 30°C."

All sound advice. Mostly.

We *do* all have a responsibility to this planet; to our home (the environment) and to our neighbours (the people, animals and ecosystems we share it with). Individual actions matter.

But when you're standing at the kitchen sink, aggressively scraping out the inside of a peanut butter jar before recycling it, while the radio reports on celebrities flying private jets, escalating military conflict, or yet another industrial pollution scandal, your jar-cleaning efforts can start to feel painfully, almost comically, insignificant.

This book isn't about that kind of sustainability.

This book examines working sustainably.

Instead of focusing solely on you as a consumer, this book focuses on you as a worker, employee, employer, freelancer, founder, or student. It helps you identify the influence your role already has, and how your everyday decisions can shape real outcomes.

This book is for the 9-to-5 crowd, the shift workers and night owls.
For restaurant managers and road workers.
For professional athletes and city bankers.
For students, graduates, and CEOs.

Whether you're just starting, early in your career and wondering *what's next*, changing direction, bored and looking for purpose, or well established and trying to make sense of what this whole "sustainability" thing actually means, this book is for you.

This book has it all.

It doesn't.

That's a lie.

I don't have all the answers. No one does.
But this book is an attempt to serve as a supportive guide; something to help you integrate sustainability into your work in ways that are practical, realistic, and relevant.

It's not about quitting your job (necessarily).
It's about changing your role from within.

It's about recognising the impact your job already has on climate and society and making more deliberate choices about how that impact shows up in the world.

How this book works

The book is split into three sections:

1. The Basics

An introduction to sustainability and climate change. It's not exhaustive, but it's everything I think you need to get started. Including the role companies play in the climate crisis, and the role individuals play *inside* those companies.

2. The Work

A practical guide to bringing sustainability into what you do every day.

Don't just read this section, *use it*.
Highlight what lands. Make notes. Capture ideas that feel relevant to your role and your industry.

This section is designed to be applied, not memorised.

3. The People

Conversations with people working in the climate space, from very different backgrounds, who found their way into this work. Alongside recommended books, podcasts, and resources for whatever comes next.

This book is built on a simple idea: no matter what you do for work, your job already has an impact on climate, often far more than you realise. *Your Job is a Climate Job* comes from a belief I've carried for a long time, and one shared by many others: that the biggest opportunity most of us have to create positive change isn't just in what we buy, but in the work we do, the systems we help shape, and the decisions we influence every day.

In Part 3 of the book, you'll meet people working across a wide range of climate-related roles and industries. Through short Q&As, we explore what their work actually looks like, how they found their way into it, and the often non-linear paths that led them there.

This book is for anyone who's ever wondered how their skills, role, or workplace might matter, and what it could look like to engage with that impact more intentionally, without needing a complete career reinvention.

Editorial Note on Terminology

Global Warming vs Climate Change

You will hear both terms used throughout this book. They are related, but not identical.

Global warming refers specifically to the long-term rise in Earth's average surface temperature caused by increased concentrations of greenhouse gases.

Climate change is broader. It includes global warming, but also the knock-on effects, such as:

- shifting rainfall patterns
- more intense storms
- rising sea levels
- melting glaciers and ice sheets

- ocean acidification
- changing ecosystems

In simple terms:
Global warming is the temperature rise.
Climate change is everything that follows from it.

The United Nations defines climate change as long-term alterations in average weather patterns and conditions. It is not about whether this summer feels hotter than last. It is about trends measured over decades.

And those trends are unmistakable.
The last decade has been the warmest on record.
Oceans are absorbing more heat than ever measured.
Sea levels are rising at accelerating rates.

Throughout this book, I will often use the word *climate* as shorthand. At times, it will stand in for broader concepts such as sustainability, environmental impact, decarbonisation, biodiversity, circular economy, and social justice. Each of these areas is distinct and complex, but they are deeply interconnected; for ease of reading, I will sometimes group them under the umbrella of "climate".

You will also see both *climate change* and *climate crisis*.

That choice is intentional.

We are in a crisis. Some describe it more accurately as a poly-crisis, where environmental breakdown interacts with social, economic, and technological pressures. The climate is changing, and the consequences are compounding.

Language shapes how we engage with both the problem and the solutions. This book does not shy away from urgency, but it also focuses on opportunity, agency, and action.

Much of the environmental damage we treat as inevitable is the result of systems we have normalised. When we question those systems, how we grow food, use land, design cities, define productivity, and allocate capital, entirely different futures become possible.

Climate work is inherently intersectional. It sits at the crossroads of:

- environmental health
- human wellbeing
- social equity
- economic resilience

Later chapters unpack this in more detail. For now, when you see the word *climate*, think of the full spectrum of sustainability work and the systems that shape how we live.

Disclaimer

Before we go any further, I want to be clear about who I am and who I'm not.

I'm not presenting myself as the world's leading expert, and I don't have all the answers. Everything I know has come from being fortunate enough to work alongside people far more experienced, knowledgeable, and resilient than I am. The ideas in this book are shaped by those who taught me, challenged me, and gave me the space to learn alongside them.

I'm deeply grateful for the opportunities I've had. I've worked with exceptional engineers, researchers, product developers, and industry specialists, across both private and public sectors, who've shaped how I think about environmental protection, standards, safety, equity and justice, energy and energy systems, emissions, and what "good" actually looks like in practice. I've learned far more from them than they'll have ever learned from me.

I also want to acknowledge the context from which I write.

This book comes from my experience working as a white man in the private sector. My perspective has been shaped by circumstance, privilege, and opportunity, including access to education, stable employment, and workplaces where I've had the time and space to reflect on sustainability alongside my core role. Not everyone has had those same conditions, and that matters.

It's also a privilege to learn about climate change rather than *experience it directly*.

For many people around the world, climate change isn't something to read about, analyse, or debate. It's already shaping daily life: failed harvests, extreme heat, flooding, displacement, loss of livelihoods, and threats to health and safety. While I observe these impacts (often from afar), I haven't been directly subjected to them in my day-to-day life. Having the time, security, and headspace to focus on learning about climate impacts is itself a position of privilege, and one that only a small portion of the global population occupies.

There are also many people working incredibly hard just to keep their heads above water, juggling long hours, unstable work, rising costs, and responsibilities at home. If that's you, I want to be clear: you are already doing an extraordinary job.

Too often, the people who keep society functioning, carers, cleaners, drivers, hospitality workers, health workers, tradespeople, and logistics staff, are the least valued and least fairly paid. We saw this starkly during COVID, particularly in the UK, where so-called "essential workers" were suddenly celebrated, but rarely compensated or supported in lasting, meaningful ways. Banging pots and pans doesn't pay their bills.

If you're stretched, exhausted, or under-resourced, the burden of fixing climate change should not fall on you. And this book isn't asking you to take on yet another responsibility.

In many ways, this book is written *because* of that reality. It's intended for those of us with more agency, security, and influence at work; the people and organisations with the power to redesign systems, make better decisions, and change the conditions that keep others undervalued or locked out of opportunity.

My hope is that this book helps shift responsibility in the right direction: away from individuals who are already carrying too much, and toward workplaces, leaders, and industries that can (and should) do better.

What follows reflects my perspective, shaped by my experiences and the people who guided me. It's not a definitive truth, and others will see things differently, and that's not only okay, but it's also necessary. I hope what's here is helpful, constructive, and offered with respect for the many people working against systems that weren't designed in their favour.

With that context, here's a little more about the people and places that shaped how I see the world, and why I believe that work can, and should, be part of the solution.

Bio

A bit about me, and why I wrote this book.
My path into sustainability didn't start with a childhood passion; I wasn't raised by 'tree-huggers', nor did I throw myself into scientific training or climate activism from a young age.
It started with selling air conditioning.
Not the origin story you'd expect.

As a student, I went to university in a British seaside town with a large student population and, in hindsight, many social issues that were hidden in plain sight.

As students, we would spend hundreds of pounds on nights out, then, drunk, leaving the clubs, eating cheesy chips and staggering back to our student accommodation laughing, while just metres away, people were sitting or sleeping on the streets. I'd seen homelessness before, but never so closely, so regularly, and in such stark contrast to how we were living. I chose to volunteer briefly at a local food bank, not because I fully understood the issue, but because it suddenly felt wrong to walk past people as if they were invisible. That feeling stayed with me, but I didn't know what to do with it or how it might connect to my work.

During my university placement year, I worked at an engineering consultancy in West Sussex (a role I was lucky to get through a connection of my mum's).[2] [3] They taught me how buildings actually work: heating systems, ventilation, insulation, and energy performance. The things most of us barely notice, yet which shape comfort, cost, health, and emissions. At the time, I did not yet grasp the climate implications, but the seed was planted. Buildings are more than structures. They shape lives.

After graduating, I joined a global air-conditioning manufacturer. It turned out to be the most formative chapter of my career. Surrounded by brilliant engineers and professionals, I was shown how to sell air conditioning and taught about building regulations, energy efficiency, refrigerants, and greenhouse gases.

Within two years, I was delivering refrigerant transition training to industry professionals, consultants, architects and contractors. While we were taught internally about the climate impacts of how we heat and cool buildings, I wanted to understand more. I was still relatively young and worried I would be out of my depth, so I read and read and read. That was when things started to shift.

Buildings account for around 40% of global greenhouse gas emissions. Electrification, replacing fossil-fuel heating for

---

[2] My mum still likely doesn't fully understand what I do for work (and that's completely fair), but she's never stopped backing me. She worked full-time while raising us, always going above and beyond to give me the opportunity and confidence to pursue work I cared about. This journey wouldn't exist without that foundation.

[3] During my engineering placement, the company director took a chance on me. I probably (definitely) brought little commercial value in that year, but he gave me time, belief and guidance. He modelled something I'll reference later in this book: that great leadership is equal parts competence and care. I'm deeply grateful for that early mentorship.

efficient electric systems, is one of the most powerful climate levers we have, and it also happened to be a solution that our business was at the forefront of.

A few years later, I moved to London and was again faced by huge levels of inequality: extreme wealth on one side of the street, deep hardship on the other.

All those early thoughts and feelings about money, food and homelessness.
All the technical work on energy, buildings, and carbon dioxide. It was the same story.

Housing is not just shelter. It is health, safety, and community, and it is one of the largest drivers of emissions on the planet. Poor quality housing traps people in hardship. Inefficient housing accelerates the climate crisis. Buildings shape both social outcomes and environmental ones.

Through my work, I had the opportunity to be involved in both private apartment developments and social housing projects with charities and trusts. I met many incredible people working across these projects, and the link between heating homes, energy efficiency, affordability, and climate became tangible and unavoidable.

In late 2023, my partner and I moved to Tāmaki Makaurau Auckland, in Aotearoa New Zealand[4]. Like many, I assumed Aotearoa New Zealand was inherently environmentally progressive, the 'greenest' of green countries. The reality is

---

[4] *Tāmaki Makaurau* is the Māori name for Auckland, and *Aotearoa* is the Māori name for New Zealand, reflecting the Indigenous language and heritage of this land.

more complex, full of challenges, and substantial opportunities. My education and work has continued; the challenges are different here compared to back home, but the end goal remains the same.

Once you start to understand the scale of the climate crisis, it becomes a one-way door. You can't go back through it, and you can't unlearn it. And I truly believe that most people do want to help, they just don't know where to start.

I'm conscious that the link between my career path and climate work might be quite clear, but through writing this book I've had the pleasure of meeting and speaking with so many people across such a wide range of sectors, many of their stories have been shared in later chapters, and the resounding conclusion I come to after speaking to every person is that;

Your job is already a climate job.

The question is whether you choose to recognise that, and what you decide to do with the influence you already have.

This book is simply the guide I wish I had when I stumbled into this work, shaped by buildings, people, carbon, inequality, opportunity, and a very roundabout journey into climate action.

PART 1: The Basics

SECTION A - The Climate Crisis

"It is well hot. Might be too hot. Might be."

As a Brit, I feel very comfortable with the weather being the safety net of small talk that Kiwis also fall back on. Moving to Aotearoa New Zealand has been like home away from home in that sense. People here love to talk about the weather.

The difference now is that it's no longer small talk.

It *is* hot.
And it's getting hotter.

What used to be a conversation filler has become a warning sign. Heat Waves. Floods. Land slips.

If you're reading this book, chances are you already know the situation we're in.
Before we talk about action, we need to understand scale.

Because the scale of corporate emissions and the systemic nature of the climate crisis are enormous, individual actions matter, but they are nowhere near enough on their own.

This book exists because the data shows that people want to act, but often don't know where to start.

There is a clear trend:

- From 2021-2025, green hiring grew twice as fast as the share of workers who have green skills [5]
- Green Transition to add 9.6 million jobs globally by 2030[6]

---

[5] LinkedIn Green Skills Report 2025
[6] World Economic Forum, Nov 2025

- 83% of people want to take climate action in their jobs[7]
- Organisations like WorkForClimate and The Climate Reality Project are already training thousands to align their careers with climate solutions.

The world of work is changing.

This book is here to help you navigate that shift, moving from *awareness* to *action*.

Because every job is a climate job.
And the question isn't *whether* your work has impact, it's what you choose to do with it.

To understand why this matters, we need to step back. Climate change is not happening in isolation; it is tangled up with biodiversity loss, ecosystem collapse, land use, food systems, and inequality.

As Hans Rosling shows in *Factfulness*, progress and crisis can coexist. The world has improved in many ways, but misunderstanding the data can leave us either paralysed by fear or falsely reassured. Climate action needs urgency, yes, but it also needs accuracy.

David MacKay makes a similar case in *Sustainable Energy without the Hot Air*. He argues that if we want to change complex systems, we first need to understand them in terms we can actually compare, measure, and plan around. His numbers-led approach cuts through slogans and wishful thinking, grounding ambition in reality.

---

[7] Kite Insights – Climate Literacy for Corporate Transformation

Together, these perspectives point to a simple but uncomfortable truth: meaningful climate action starts not with how strongly we feel, but with how well we understand the system we are trying to change.

So, before we get into the science, a quick warning: there's no Margot Robbie in a bubble bath or Anthony Bourdain explaining the Global Financial Crisis, as we saw in Adam McKay's *The Big Short*. Here, however, you're stuck with me (I didn't have the budget for Ryan Gosling), so please bear with me through the following few pages as we break down the climate basics.

Climate Emergency

The Earth is naturally warmed by something called the greenhouse effect. Without it, the planet would be a frozen rock, roughly 33°C colder than it is today. Life as we know it would not exist.

Here's how it works.

The sun sends energy to Earth in the form of shortwave radiation. Some of that energy is reflected back into space by clouds, ice, and bright surfaces. The rest is absorbed by the land and oceans, warming the planet. The Earth then releases that energy back toward space as longwave infrared radiation.

Certain gases in the atmosphere trap some of that outgoing heat. They absorb and re-emit it in all directions, including back toward the Earth's surface. This creates a natural insulating blanket that keeps temperatures stable enough for life.

That insulating process is the greenhouse effect. It's essential (so not inherently bad).

The problem is not the greenhouse effect itself.
The problem is that we are thickening the blanket.

The gases responsible for trapping heat are called greenhouse gases. The main ones are:

• Carbon dioxide (CO_2), largely from burning coal, oil, and gas, and from deforestation
• Methane (CH_4), from livestock, fossil fuel extraction, and waste
• Nitrous oxide (N_2O), mainly from fertilisers and industrial processes
• Other fluorinated gases, from refrigeration and industrial uses

It's worth clarifying here that the ozone layer is Earth's natural UV shield, absorbing harmful radiation high in the atmosphere. Ozone-depleting gases, chemicals such as chlorofluorocarbons (CFCs) damaged this shield, increasing risks of skin cancer and ecological harm, particularly over Antarctica. Greenhouse gases like CO_2 and methane, however, work differently; they trap heat near the surface, driving global warming. One problem lets in more radiation. The other traps more heat. Both are serious, but they operate through different mechanisms.

Carbon dioxide is the most talked about because it is emitted in vast quantities and stays in the atmosphere for a very long time, often hundreds of years. Methane is emitted in smaller amounts but is far more potent in the short term, trapping much more heat on a molecule-for-molecule basis.

NASA visualisations show this clearly. When you look at satellite data over time, you can literally see carbon dioxide concentrations rising year after year, thickening that atmospheric blanket.

Since the Industrial Revolution, human activity has increased atmospheric CO_2 concentrations by roughly 50%. According to the United Nations and the IPCC, these levels are higher than at any point in at least 800,000 years.

That is not a small nudge to the system. That is a structural shift.

When we talk about emissions, carbon budgets, and pathways to 1.5°C, we are talking about how much more we are willing to thicken that atmospheric blanket. Every tonne of carbon dioxide added increases the concentration in the atmosphere. A significant portion will remain there for centuries. The system responds to the total stock, not just the latest flow.

This is why historic emissions matter. And it is why climate change is fundamentally a systems issue. Energy systems, land use, food production, transport, buildings, industry, finance, and consumption patterns all feed into greenhouse gas levels.

Understanding the greenhouse effect grounds the rest of this book. It strips away slogans and brings us back to physics. We are not debating opinions. We are altering the composition of the atmosphere.

It is also worth acknowledging something you will often hear: "But the climate has always changed."

That part is true.

Over hundreds of thousands, even millions, of years, Earth's temperature has naturally risen and fallen. Ice ages have come and gone. Warm periods have expanded and contracted. These shifts were driven by slow changes in Earth's orbit, volcanic activity, and natural carbon cycles.

Humans have been around for roughly 300,000 years and have lived through dramatic shifts in climate, including multiple ice ages. Entire ice sheets advanced and retreated. Sea levels rose and fell. Landscapes transformed. Early humans survived not because conditions were stable, but because they adapted.

One of the most important tools we had was mobility. When climates shifted, humans migrated. We moved toward warmer regions, toward reliable water sources, toward landscapes that could still support food and shelter. Small populations could relocate when conditions became harsh.

But two things matter here: speed and context.

First, speed. Past climate shifts unfolded over thousands of years. What we are seeing now is happening over decades. According to the IPCC, the current rate of warming is unprecedented in at least the last 2,000 years, and likely far longer. Ecosystems and human systems struggle not just with change, but with rapid change.

Second, context. During the last ice age, global human population was measured in the millions, not billions. Today we are more than eight billion people living within fixed national borders, urban infrastructure, agricultural systems, and complex geopolitical arrangements. Most of us cannot simply migrate when temperatures rise or rainfall patterns collapse. Food systems are globally interconnected. Water resources are already under pressure. Governments manage borders tightly. Conflict, inequality, and political instability shape who can move and who cannot.

Yes, humanity has survived climate shifts before. But never with this many people. Never this quickly. And never within such tightly interdependent economic and political systems.

When people say "climate change will end the planet," that is not quite accurate. The planet will be fine. Earth has survived asteroid impacts, supervolcanoes, and mass extinctions.

What is at risk are the living systems on it. Stable coastlines. Freshwater supplies. Food systems. Biodiversity. Humans. You and me.

The asteroid that wiped out the dinosaurs did not kill them instantly on impact. The collision triggered cascading effects: shockwaves, global fires, debris blocking sunlight, dramatic temperature shifts, and the collapse of food chains. It was the chain reaction that proved catastrophic. Life did not end entirely, but roughly 75% of species disappeared. That's no small number.

Climate change works in a similar way. Rising temperatures trigger feedback loops: melting ice reduces reflectivity, warming oceans release stored carbon, drought fuels wildfires, ecosystems destabilise, food systems strain, migration increases, and political tensions rise. It is not one event. It is a cascade.

Understanding that shifts the narrative. This is not about saving the planet in some abstract sense. It is about protecting the conditions that make civilisation, biodiversity, and daily life possible.

And those conditions are changing faster than most systems were built to handle.

Once you understand that, carbon emissions stop being abstract numbers and start being what they are: additional heat retained in the system that supports every ecosystem, economy, and community on Earth.

Global greenhouse gas emissions reached a record 53.2 gigatonnes of carbon dioxide equivalent ($GtCO_2$-e) in 2024, up around 1.3% from 2023 (IEA, Global Energy Review 2024).

A gigatonne is a billion tonnes. And one tonne of CO_2 gas is about 8 metres wide, long, and tall. That is taller than a typical two-storey house.

With a world population now above eight billion, total emissions continue rising even as governments commit, on paper, to decarbonisation.

Most emissions still come from a small number of major economies (IPCC AR6, 2023). The Intergovernmental Panel on Climate Change is the United Nations body that assesses global climate science, effectively acting as the world's climate "VAR system," reviewing thousands of peer-reviewed studies before calling the facts.

Meanwhile, the harshest consequences fall on regions least responsible: Sub-Saharan Africa, low-lying islands, South Asia, and Arctic communities. They are already experiencing sea-level rise, extreme weather, and ecological disruption.

The science is clear. Fossil fuel combustion, deforestation, and industrial processes have driven greenhouse gas levels to concentrations unprecedented in hundreds of thousands of years.[8]

Biodiversity loss is accelerating too. WWF's Living Planet Report 2022 reports that wildlife populations have declined by roughly 69% since 1970, and nearly one million species face extinction.[9]

Climate breakdown and biodiversity collapse are not parallel crises. They amplify one another.

As Yvon Chouinard writes in *Let My People Go Surfing*, the economy is a wholly owned subsidiary of the environment. Push nature beyond its limits, and everything resting on it becomes unstable.

Every year, we continue to set records for temperature extremes, flooding, wildfires, drought, and climate-driven displacement. Entire ecosystems are collapsing. Some scientists compare the scale of biodiversity loss to the aftermath of the asteroid that wiped out the dinosaurs, only this time, we are the asteroid.

The Global South is bearing the brunt of climate breakdown despite being the least responsible for its causes.

---

[8] IPCC AR6, WG1, 2021
[9] Global Assessment Report on Biodiversity and Ecosystem Services, IPBES, 2019

As Natalie Kyriacou writes in *Nature's Last Dance*, every lost species or damaged habitat is a story ended. Climate action is fundamentally about protecting lives and stories.

This is not abstract crisis talk. It is the backdrop to your working life, your skills, and the jobs that will exist in the decades ahead.

The Paris Agreement

The Paris Agreement's commitment to keep warming *"well below 2°C"* and to pursue efforts to limit it to *1.5°C* was never symbolic. Recent research shows that the Earth is already temporarily breaching the 1.5°C threshold during individual years and months, mainly driven by ongoing emissions and natural variability. While this does not yet constitute a permanent breach of the Paris Agreement target (which is measured over longer-term averages), it underscores how close the climate system already is to 1.5°C, and how narrow the remaining margin for action has become.[10] Every decimal of warming matters.

The difference between 1.5°C and 2°C of global warming is not just a number. At 2°C, heatwaves, droughts and heavy rainfall events become more frequent and intense, exposing more people and regions to water stress, flooding and overlapping climate risks. Food and water security, health, infrastructure and livelihoods all face significantly higher pressure, while

---

[10] *The Conversation "Earth is already shooting through the 1.5°C global warming limit" (2024).*

ecosystems experience greater loss and disruption. Limiting warming closer to 1.5°C reduces these risks, supports adaptation and protects more of the natural systems that communities depend on.[11]

These are no longer hypothetical trends; they are happening now.

In the UK, the National Risk Register 2025 explicitly includes climate-related risks such as heatwaves, storms, flooding, and wildfires as evolving and material threats to society, infrastructure, and services — reflecting a shift from what "could" happen to what *is* happening as climate impacts intensify. The updated register also incorporates a new chronic risks analysis that includes climate change among the most critical long-term challenges facing the nation. These assessments underscore direct impacts on health, infrastructure, and economic stability while warning that adaptation and resilience efforts must accelerate alongside mitigation.

Despite the scale of the crisis, progress has been made.

A decade on from the Paris Agreement, UN Secretary-General António Guterres has argued that two things can be true at once: *Paris is working, and it is nowhere near enough.*

When nearly every country on Earth signed the agreement in 2015, it created the first truly global, legally binding framework to reduce emissions and adapt to climate impacts. Ten years later, although the last decade has been the hottest on record, the world is no longer on a trajectory toward more than 4°C of

---

[11] IPCC 2025

warming, a scenario widely considered unlivable. Current pathways sit closer to around 2.5°C.

That shift matters. It reflects hard-won progress driven by policy, technology, activism, and market change. Paris helped unlock a global clean-energy transformation: solar and wind are scaling at record speed, costs have plummeted, and new industries and jobs are emerging. Cities, regions, businesses, and communities are often moving faster than national governments.

But progress is not victory.

Science tells us that a temporary overshoot of 1.5°C is now likely to occur in the early 2030s. What remains within our control is the depth and duration of that overshoot, and whether we act fast enough to bring temperatures back down. That will depend on accelerating action across ambition, adaptation, and finance.

For Aotearoa New Zealand and the Pacific, the difference between 1.5°C and 2°C is between disruption and an existential threat.

Impacts include sea-level rise and flooding, saltwater intrusion affecting water security, more intense cyclones and rainfall, and rising heat stress on vulnerable communities.[12]

Across the Pacific, climate communication is shifting from polar bears to people, land, culture, and community.

---

[12] NIWA, *Climate Change Projections for New Zealand*, 2023; IPCC AR6 Regional Chapters, 2022.

Paris is not an aspiration. It is a safety boundary. And staying within it now depends less on distant promises and more on implementation across energy systems, infrastructure, finance, and the everyday decisions made in workplaces worldwide.

Individual vs. Corporate impact.

What about our place in all of this?

Let's assume you could go completely off-grid, eat kale for breakfast, lunch and dinner, plant a small forest in your backyard, and recycle like your life depends on it.

Unfortunately, global emissions would barely notice.

Why? Because the primary drivers of climate change are not individuals; they are the corporations that power the fossil fuel economy, industrial agriculture, and unsustainable production systems.

Yet we've been sold a convenient myth: that our most significant leverage lies in being consumers.

We're told:

- *Recycle like a responsible member of the community.*
- *Turn off lights in rooms you're not using and only wash clothes at 30°C to save energy.*
- *Buy an EV so children can breathe clean air on your street*

All of which is sound advice, but it ignores the structural reality: in many cases, consumers don't have meaningful choices.

In many countries, renewable energy isn't widely available, or fossil fuel companies control the price.

Many supermarkets still don't offer affordable plant-based alternatives.

Michael Pollan's The Omnivore's Dilemma reveals how even simple choices, such as what we eat, are shaped by vast systems, a helpful reminder that individual climate action always sits within a larger structural context.

Government policy, infrastructure, and corporate power shape what "choices" people get in the first place. Even publishing this book on Amazon reflects that reality; it holds a near-monopoly over global book distribution and thus, remains one of the few ways for an independent publisher to reach readers at scale. This is an acknowledgement of how embedded these systems are.

The system is designed for consumption. We, as individuals and consumers, still have agency, but blaming consumers completely is convenient and strategically misleading.

And that brings us to one of the most overlooked truths in climate work: your most significant influence usually isn't in what you buy, it's in what you build, design, approve, challenge, manage, fund, or lead through your job.

What can you do that has an impact? As a consumer, your actions can help by reducing consumption, travelling low-carbon when possible (active or public transport), choosing plant-based foods, and selecting ethical investments. These things matter, but they are the tip of the iceberg. Recent reports show that the impact of individual behaviour is *massively overestimated* without system-wide change.[13]

The real power is your work and influence.

The most significant influence most people have is through their jobs:

- Choose where you work. Does the company add value to society or profit from environmental destruction?
- Ask questions. If you recycle at home, why work for a company that generates a ton of non-recyclable waste? Spending most of your life working for a company that contradicts your values.
- Use your voice. If you can't leave, influence from within. Ask about the company's environmental strategy. Bring colleagues together. Show your leadership team that people care and expect better.

We're told that capitalism "Follows consumer demand," but reality paints a different picture.

Governments subsidise fossil fuel companies, allow monopolies to flourish and create false markets where "choice" is an illusion.

Grace Blakeley's *Vulture Capitalism* argues that what we call "modern capitalism" is no longer primarily about markets, competition, or innovation. It's about power, who holds it, who protects it, and who benefits when things go wrong.

---

[13] "The Most Impactful Things You Can Do for the Climate Aren't What You've Been Told" World Resources Institute, 2025.

When a small number of firms dominate housing, energy, food, transport, or finance, individual choice becomes a narrative convenience rather than a real lever of change.

Take the UK's public transport: Many people face a "choice" between low-cost domestic flights and prohibitively expensive, unreliable rail. That's not the free market at work; that's policy failure.

Many political leaders still underestimate public concern about environmental issues, even as lobbying from private interests delays progress.

However, as workers, employees, leaders, and business owners, we can drive positive change from within by influencing decisions, shifting priorities, and changing corporate culture.

If systems are built and maintained by organisations, then the most meaningful leverage most people have is through their work, not their shopping basket.

Corporations shape the world, not consumers.

According to the CDP Carbon Majors Report (2017), 100 active fossil fuel producers have been responsible for 71% of global industrial greenhouse gas emissions since 1988 (the year the IPCC formally recognised human-induced climate change).

At the time of this publication, COP30 (Belém, Brazil - November 2025) has just wrapped up, with an agreement that doesn't explicitly mention cutting fossil fuels. On a separate, and completely unrelated note, more than 1,600 fossil fuel lobbyists have been granted access to the COP30 climate negotiations (meaning that one in every 25 participants is a fossil fuel lobbyist).

For reference, COP stands for the Conference of the Parties. It is the annual United Nations climate summit where nearly every country on Earth meets to negotiate, review progress, and argue about how to respond to climate change. If climate politics were a workplace, COP would be the biggest, messiest annual all-hands meeting: everyone shows up, everyone brings different priorities, the agenda is ambitious, progress is slow, and nothing gets done without compromise.

A relatively small group of fossil fuel and industrial producers dominate global emissions. We will come back to who they are later, but for now, the critical point is this: climate change is driven far more by the systems we work in than by any one person's shopping basket. These organisations (state-owned and investor-owned alike) could dramatically shift the trajectory of climate change. Many have the capital, expertise, and influence to lead the transition. Yet too often, climate progress is delayed in pursuit of short-term profit.

This isn't just about *what we buy.*
It's about the systems we support with our labour, creativity, and time.
The decisions made in boardrooms, engineering teams, investment committees, and design meetings have far greater influence than those made at supermarket checkouts.

We need to stop seeing ourselves as powerless consumers.
We are workers. Decision-makers. Investors. Humans.
And the organisations we help build today shape the world we, and future generations, will inherit tomorrow.

A call to action

- Ask yourself: *What kind of company do I want to work for?*
- Ask your employer: *What are we doing to reduce our environmental impact? How do we contribute positively to society?*
- Act: Use your influence; in your team, your company, your investments, or your community.

By shifting the narrative from passive consumption to active participation, we can have a far greater impact on our collective future.

This is not about shifting responsibility from 'ourselves' to 'others'—but about recognising accountability must be shared: individual and systemic.

In *Moral Ambition*, Rutger Bregman makes an important distinction. Yes, corporations and governments must be held accountable for the harm they cause. But that truth does not absolve the rest of us of responsibility. Recognising structural failure is not the same as opting out of agency.

Bregman argues that much of modern climate morality has focused on minimising harm: flying less, consuming less, leaving as small a footprint as possible. Those choices matter, but they are not the ceiling of what's possible. A life spent trying to leave no trace is very different from a life spent trying to leave things better. His challenge is simple and uncomfortable: don't just aim to *not* make things worse, aim to make things better.

That means being ambitious. It means aligning parts of your career, skills, and energy toward creating positive impact, ripple effects, and the occasional butterfly effect. It means learning how systems work, engaging with people and communities, getting involved in real problems, and helping build real solutions. You don't have to do it alone, and you don't have to do everything. But choosing ambition, however imperfect, is very different from opting out. And in a world shaped by collective action, it is far more powerful than putting your head in the sand.

The Housing Climate

There is one system most of us feel in our bones: housing.

In my bio, I touched on the emotions attached to seeing people experiencing homelessness. It's hard not to notice. You walk past someone sleeping in a doorway, and the big flowery policy language about "economic systems" disappears. This is not a spreadsheet problem. It's a human one.

Homelessness sits at the sharpest edge of a much wider crisis.

In the UK, hundreds of thousands of people are in temporary accommodation or without secure housing, and rough sleeping has risen significantly in recent years.[14] In Australia, more than 120,000 people were recorded as experiencing homelessness on Census night, with many more living in overcrowded or unstable conditions. In Aotearoa New Zealand, tens of thousands are considered severely housing deprived, including people living in cars, garages, emergency accommodation, or

---

[14] Homelessness: causes, types and facts. Crisis.

overcrowded homes.[15] Rough sleeping is only the visible fraction of a much deeper problem.

Homelessness is not caused by housing costs alone. There are many complex social drivers, but housing supply, affordability, and stability matter enormously. When safe, affordable homes are out of reach, vulnerability increases. Housing stress and homelessness are connected, even if they are not identical.

And this crisis stretches far beyond those sleeping rough.

In many countries, renting is the norm. In others, owning a home is still treated as the ultimate milestone of adulthood. For my parents' generation in the UK, having a spouse, children and a house in your thirties was considered normal. If you didn't own by 30, you were "late to the party." Now, buying a home in your thirties is often seen as an extraordinary achievement, usually requiring dual incomes, years of sacrifice (no more Netflix or avocado on toast), or an inheritance.

Access to housing has drifted out of reach for many. Prices have risen far faster than wages. Rents consume disproportionate shares of income. Meanwhile, in the UK and elsewhere, large organisations and overseas investors own growing numbers of properties, and institutional capital increasingly treats housing as an asset class rather than a social foundation. Governments promise to build more homes, while hundreds of thousands of properties sit empty.

Something about that feels broken.

---

[15] Orange Sky, New Zealand.

Housing has quietly shifted from being a basic human need to being treated primarily as a financial instrument, a retirement strategy, a vehicle for capital growth. Call me an idealistic hippie if you like, but I think housing should be accessible. It should not exist mainly to inflate pension pots.

And here's why this belongs in a climate book.

Homes are more than shelter. They shape whether you sleep well. Whether your children wake up coughing. Whether you feel safe. Whether you dread winter because of the power bill. Whether you can build a sense of community.

The quality of a home affects health, stress levels and finances. It determines how much you pay to stay warm. Whether walls are damp. Whether mould keeps returning. Whether you are forced to live miles from work because that is all you can afford, locking you into long commutes and higher emissions.

Housing shapes everyday life. It influences energy use, heating systems, insulation standards, materials, land use and transport patterns. A warm, efficient home lowers bills and reduces emissions. A cold, leaky one does the opposite.

And most of our housing stock is not fit for the future.

In the UK, homes are among the least energy-efficient in Europe. The average UK house price in 2004 was around £150,000. In 2024 it sits closer to £280,000–£300,000 nationally, and far higher in some regions. Yet many of those homes have seen little meaningful upgrade in insulation, ventilation or heating systems. On paper they are worth more. In reality, many perform poorly and cost more to run each year.

In Aotearoa New Zealand, over 20% of homes are reported as damp or mouldy. Nearly 1 in 10 households have taken out loans to pay energy bills. Cold, inefficient housing is not just uncomfortable. It is expensive, unhealthy and unfair.

Something is not right.

Governments do not necessarily need to fund every retrofit themselves. But they do need to fix the rules of the game. Stronger building standards. Clear energy performance disclosure. Incentives for retrofit and electrification. Planning reform that supports well-designed density. Policies that treat housing as essential infrastructure, not simply speculative property.

And there are examples of doing it better.

Singapore's public housing system houses more than 80% of its population through long-term state-supported programmes that treat housing as nation-building infrastructure rather than just private investment. Denmark's social housing model, run by non-profit housing associations with strong municipal support, provides affordable, stable homes to a broad cross-section of society rather than only the very poorest. Different systems. Different cultures. But both recognise that housing stability underpins social stability.

This is where your role comes back into focus.

If you work in construction, architecture, engineering, planning, finance, property, interiors, energy, or local government, this is climate work. Deep retrofit. Insulation. Ventilation. Electrification. Heat pumps. Better materials. Smarter design.

Maybe you have spent years designing kitchens, bathrooms and toilets. Maybe you are a surveyor, electrician, project manager or mortgage advisor. Your skills do not disappear. They evolve. Perhaps now is the time to upskill into retrofit advisory work. To help people improve the homes they already live in. To deliver comfort, lower bills, and cut emissions at the same time.

This links back to a theme we will return to: assess where you can add value. Not everyone needs to start again from scratch. Often, the most powerful shift is redirecting your existing skills toward better outcomes.

Housing is climate.

Improving it is some of the most practical, tangible climate work there is. Work that improves housing quality, affordability, retrofit standards, insulation, electrification, tenancy rights or planning reform is climate work. Work that supports social housing, community-led development or challenges speculative hoarding of homes is climate work.

This issue is deeply personal and interconnected. It affects people sleeping rough, families in overcrowded rentals, young professionals locked out of ownership, and older generations worried about security in retirement. It cuts across class, generation and geography.

And like so many climate issues, it reminds us of something important: this is not about whether you recycle your coffee cup.

It is about the structures we build and maintain.

If you work in property, planning, finance, construction, policy, investment or local government, your job shapes housing outcomes. If you work elsewhere but vote, invest or influence conversations, you are still part of the system.

Housing is not a side issue. It is a climate issue.

Who's Driving Emissions?

The uncomfortable truth is that global climate action has lagged far behind the science for decades. We emitted more greenhouse gases in the twenty years after the Kyoto Protocol than in the twenty years before it, despite knowing far more about the risks (UNFCCC Historical Emissions Dataset, 2022). And while the Paris Agreement set an ambition to limit warming to 1.5°C, no major industrialised nation is currently on a pathway consistent with that goal (UNEP, Emissions Gap Report 2024).

This gap between ambition and action is impossible to ignore at international climate summits. COP conferences are often framed as moments of global leadership, yet they continue to attract fossil fuel lobbyists in staggering numbers.

At COP29 in Baku, 1,773 fossil fuel lobbyists were registered. At COP30 in Belém, the figure was estimated at approximately 1,600, representing roughly one in every twenty-five attendees. In both cases, draft negotiation texts did not explicitly mention oil, gas, or coal. Even as civil society and Indigenous groups pushed hard for stronger commitments, including the Fossil

Fuel Non-Proliferation Treaty, influence consistently lagged behind representation.

The pattern repeated itself across negotiations. At COP29, civil society groups called for a "just and full phase-out" of fossil fuels, but no binding commitment emerged. At COP30, early draft texts omitted fossil fuels entirely, and final language remained vague despite public pressure. Industry influence was particularly visible through the promotion of carbon capture, utilisation, and storage (CCS), with hundreds of lobbyists advocating for technologies critics argue risk prolonging fossil fuel dependence rather than ending it. In fact, at COP30, fossil fuel lobbyists outnumbered nearly every national delegation except Brazil's.

None of this reflects a lack of knowledge. As Nathaniel Rich documents in *Losing Earth*, the tragedy of climate change is not ignorance, but delay. By the late 1980s, the science was clear, and the solutions were known. What failed was not understanding, but political will.

That history matters because it explains where we are now. It reminds us that progress has never been blocked by a shortage of evidence, but by power, incentives, and who gets a seat at the table — and who does not.

It's worth recognising something that is often overlooked in the climate narrative: the systems driving the crisis today are the same systems that enabled much of the world's economic progress over the past century. Plastics and fossil fuels, for all their catastrophic environmental impacts, have also played undeniable roles in human development. Plastics have enabled advances in modern medicine, food safety, clean water distribution, laboratory research, electronics, and global logistics. Fossil fuels powered the industrial era, expanded access to heating and cooling, enabled population growth and economic expansion, and supported manufacturing, mobility, and many of the comforts that billions rely on today.

However, these benefits came at a cost, and they were never distributed evenly. In Jeremy Williams' book, *Climate Change Is Racist*, he outlines that the same systems that created prosperity for some created extraction, pollution, and instability for others. Many communities that contributed the least to global emissions were exploited for resources, displaced for infrastructure, or exposed to pollution exported by wealthier nations. For every society lifted by industrialisation, others were pushed to its margins. Development for some was made possible through the dispossession of others.

This is why climate justice cannot be separated from climate science. What some nations view as "progress", others experience as the loss of land, health, biodiversity, cultural continuity, and future opportunities. The historical emissions ledger tells only part of the story. The social ledger tells the rest.

Acknowledging this duality, that fossil fuels and plastics brought genuine benefits while also driving profound harm, is essential if we are to design a fair and effective transition. We cannot simply condemn the past or romanticise it.

We must recognise that the systems we inherited were built on extractive logics: take, use, dispose. Burn now, address consequences later. Build the economy, ignore the ecology.

Measure GDP growth while externalising environmental and social damage.

Those logics are still embedded today. Most people don't choose plastic; they are handed a system in which alternatives are inaccessible, unaffordable, or non-existent. Most people don't actively select fossil fuels; they live in energy systems, cities, transport networks, and housing stock built around dependence on fossil fuels. Consumer choice is limited because the system was not designed to support it.

This is why the solution cannot rest solely on individual action. We need structural shifts: in how products are designed, how energy is generated, how companies are regulated, how natural capital is valued (or ignored), and how economies define success. Continuing with business-as-usual, endless extraction and perpetual GDP growth, is incompatible with planetary boundaries and ultimately incompatible with human wellbeing.

The task ahead isn't simply to reduce harm; it's to redesign the systems that caused it. That means moving towards circularity, regenerative economic models, low-carbon infrastructure, and governance that finally values nature as the foundation of human life, not an optional extra. It also means ensuring that the transition does not repeat past injustices but corrects them, redistributing benefits and reducing burdens in ways that respect culture, community, and equity.

Only by acknowledging both the gains and the harms of the last century can we build systems that uplift rather than exploit. Systems shaped not by extraction, but by responsibility, repair, and resilience.

What remains indisputable is this:
The nations least responsible for climate change will remain the earliest and most severely affected.

And that is precisely why understanding your *carbon footprint* (and handprint, and *climate shadow – more on this later)* matters, because the systems shaping our world (including global climate policy) don't change quickly on their own.

They change when people, individuals, professionals, voters, workers, and leaders push them to do so.

The most significant contributors to greenhouse gas (GHG) emissions are not individual consumers but rather a relatively small number of fossil-fuel and industrial producers.

Earlier, we saw that a small number of producers dominate global emissions. The Carbon Majors Database quantifies this reality and shows that just 100 fossil fuel and cement companies are responsible for approximately 71% of global industrial GHG emissions since 1988. These emissions include both direct operational emissions and downstream emissions from the combustion of the fuels they supply. The leading contributors include:

1. Saudi Aramco – world's largest oil producer (state-owned)
2. Gazprom – Russian state-controlled gas company
3. National Iranian Oil Company (NIOC) – major oil and gas producer
4. ExxonMobil – U.S. investor-owned multinational
5. PetroChina – part of China National Petroleum Corporation
6. BP – UK-based multinational
7. Shell – Anglo-Dutch energy company
8. Chevron – U.S. multinational corporation
9. Pemex – Mexico's state-owned petroleum company
10. ConocoPhillips – U.S. multinational

It is estimated that around 90% of these companies' emissions arise from the use of their products rather than from their direct operations.

More recent studies reinforce this trend. In 2023, only 36 major energy producers accounted for half of global fossil CO_2 emissions, underscoring that a disproportionately small number of companies continue to drive a significant share of climate impact.

Understanding this concentration is critical: climate change is not simply the result of individual choices, but of systemic dependence on high-emission industrial sectors. Effective solutions must therefore target transformation across energy systems, supply chains, and policy, not just personal consumption.

Are we locked into these systems? Is a transition to renewable energy sources possible, or are we hopelessly trying in vain?

Anyone who's been watching Landman may recall Billy Bob Thorntons character, Tommy Norris, famously saying (about wind turbines) *"Do you have any idea how much diesel they have to burn to mix the concrete or make that steel? Or haul this shit out here, and put it together with a 450-foot crane? You want to guess how much oil it takes to lubricate that fucking thing, or winterize it? In its 20-year lifespan, it won't offset the carbon footprint of making it. And don't get me started on solar panels and the lithium in your Tesla battery..."*.

The reality is that Tommy Norris was wrong, by a magnitude of roughly 25 to 1. In real life, modern wind turbines typically repay the carbon used to build them within months, not decades, and then spend the rest of their operating life producing near-zero-carbon electricity. It makes for a powerful monologue, but it is built on outdated assumptions rather than current evidence.

Although these corporations are primarily accountable, responsibility does not end with them. We must advocate for policy and corporate change while also striving, individually, to align our careers, influence, and decisions with solutions, not just emissions. As Bregman argues in *Moral Ambition*, meaningful impact often begins with where we choose to put our talent.

All of this leads to a simple but crucial question: what does climate action actually cost, and what is the cost of doing nothing?

The Climate Cost

Rather than weakening corporate power, crises often entrench it, leaving societies more unequal and less resilient than before.

When we talk about the "cost" of climate policy, it's easy to picture climate action as a giant new bill landing on the global doormat. But the real choice isn't *"pay for climate action or save money"*. It's *"pay to transform our energy and infrastructure in a planned way now, or pay far more later in disaster clean-up, crop failures, health costs, and instability."*

How much will net zero actually cost?

Big picture: getting to 'net zero' is about redirecting investment, not inventing an entirely new pot of money.

McKinsey estimates that the world will need to invest approximately US\$9.2 trillion annually on physical assets for the net-zero transition between now and 2050, up from about US\$5.7 trillion today.[16] That's an increase of roughly US\$3.5 trillion a year, equivalent to around 7.5% of global GDP, much

---

[16] McKinsey Global Institute: The Net Zero Transition 2022

of which is money we would be spending anyway on energy, buildings, vehicles and industry, just in a dirtier way.

The International Monetary Fund (IMF) looked at the macro-economic effect of strong climate policies and concluded that, with well-designed measures, the impact on global growth would be modest: on the order of 1–1.5% of global GDP in 2030[17], or a reduction of about 0.15 percentage points in annual growth through mid-century, *while* avoiding catastrophic climate damages.

In other words: serious climate policy is not "ending the economy"; it's roughly in the same economic ballpark as other big public choices we already make.

For comparison, countries spend, on average, about 4–5% of GDP on education and about 2.3% of global GDP on the military each year.[18] Climate and nature investment sit in that exact order of magnitude. It's big – but not bigger than things we already fund without question.

And how much does *inaction* cost?

This is where the numbers get uncomfortable.

A recent analysis from Boston Consulting Group warns that unchecked climate change could wipe out around 13% of global GDP by 2100[19] – far more than the cost of transition. The Investor Group on Climate Change has estimated that delaying the renewable energy transition could reduce global GDP by US$6–8 trillion by 2050, as climate damages and lost opportunities compound.

---

[17] IMF Reaching Net Zero Emissions 2021

[18] World Bank Open Data, World Bank Group, 2025
[19] Forbes: Climate Inaction 2025

We're already seeing what those damages look like in practice:

- Munich Re reports that natural disasters caused around US$320 billion in economic losses in 2024, up from US$268 billion in 2023, with only part of that insured.
- Swiss Re notes that insured losses from natural catastrophes have exceeded US$100 billion every year for four years running, mainly driven by weather and climate-related events.
- The 2024–25 Asia floods have already killed thousands and caused tens of billions of dollars in damage across South and Southeast Asia, displacing millions of people and exposing how fragile critical infrastructure is when resilience hasn't been adequately funded.

And this is before we fully price in slower-burn impacts: lower agricultural yields, heat-related productivity loss, health impacts, migration, and damage to ecosystems that underpin our economies.

So, the rough story is:

Serious climate policy might cost 1–2% of GDP per year. Unchecked climate damage risks 5–13% (or more) of GDP by the end of the century.

Each 1°C increase in global temperature can be linked to a 12% decline in global GDP, according to the report by the National Bureau of Economic Research.

From a purely economic angle, *doing nothing* is the expensive option.

Adaptation, loss, and damage – who pays? Even if we achieve net zero, a certain amount of warming and disruption is already locked in. The UN estimates that adaptation costs in developing countries alone could reach US$140–300 billion per year by 2030, rising further to US$300–600 billion by 2050.

These are countries that have contributed least to the problem and yet face some of the highest bills: reinforcing coastlines, upgrading housing, shifting agriculture, protecting water supplies, and responding to more frequent disasters. In the Pacific and across Aotearoa's wider neighbourhood, this isn't an abstract future; it's evacuation plans, damaged homes, and saltwater in drinking water.

That's why climate economics is also a justice question: who pays for adaptation, and who pays for the loss and damage that can't be adapted to? Currently, far too much of that cost falls on already strained national budgets and local communities.

Meanwhile... we're still subsidising the problem.

Here's the twist: while we argue about whether we can "afford" climate action, we continue to pour eye-watering sums into the very fuels driving the crisis.

The IMF estimates that *total* fossil fuel subsidies (including under-pricing of climate and health damage) reached about US$7 trillion globally in 2022.

Even if you only count explicit consumer subsidies, the IEA found these hit a *record* US$1.3 trillion in 2022, as governments stepped in to shield households from high fossil fuel prices rather than speeding the switch to clean energy[20].

So, when we ask, "How will we pay for net zero?", one honest answer is:
Let's start by stopping paying to make the problem worse.

Phasing out fossil fuel subsidies, closing tax loopholes, and ending special treatment for high-emitting sectors would free up vast sums for: clean energy and public transport; climate-resilient infrastructure; support for workers and communities

---

[20] IEA Net Zero by 2050, 2021.

transitioning out of fossil-fuel-dependent industries; and loss and damage funds for countries already on the front line.

None of that is politically easy. But it is economically coherent.

If you zoom out, climate investment is not a novel category. It's infrastructure, housing, transport, water, food systems and energy – the basics of a functioning society – redesigned to survive in a hotter, more volatile world.

We already accept that:

- Education is worth 4–5% of GDP because it builds human potential.
- Health is worth another substantial slice because it keeps people alive and productive.
- Defence is worth 2–3% of GDP because governments want to manage security risks.

Climate and nature investment sits alongside these: it protects the physical and ecological systems on which everything else depends. It's not a "nice to have". It's risk management, resilience, and long-term value creation.

The hard part isn't the maths; it's the politics. Redirecting a few per cent of global GDP means changing who wins, who loses, and who no longer gets tax breaks. It means saying no to some very powerful incumbents. It means designing fair transitions, so workers in fossil fuel and high-emission sectors are supported, retrained, and not simply discarded.

But from a purely economic lens, the conclusion is pretty simple:

We will pay for climate change one way or another.
The only real choice is whether we invest upfront in a planned transition,

Or keep writing ever-larger cheques for disasters, losses, and instability.

And that is where your job, your industry, and your organisation come in. The decisions being made in boardrooms, design studios, council chambers, classrooms, and control rooms will determine whether we treat climate policy as a drag on growth or as one of the smartest investments of this century.

When we talk about affordability, these are the numbers that matter most. Not whether individuals recycle perfectly, but whether our economic systems keep funding the problem instead of the solution.

As Peter Frankopan argues in *The Earth Transformed*, societies rise and fall not only through war and economics but also through how well they manage their relationship with the planet. Including this environmental dimension reminds us that climate action isn't a modern add-on; it's part of a pattern stretching back through history.

And that is precisely why your job, whatever it is, becomes part of the story. The transition is happening, but the speed and fairness of that transition depends on the decisions we make in our workplaces every day.

Climate Myth-Busting

Some common claims in the media and on social media distort the science. Here are facts, informed by Shachar Hatan at Climate Impact Partners:

"I'm not a climate scientist, but..."
That's precisely why we listen to climate scientists. Dismissing

climate action as a "social contagion" or claiming it's driven by "narcissistic psychopaths" insults both science and the communities already impacted. Climate science is rigorous, peer-reviewed, and about measured risk management.

"The Earth is in a cooling period."
Misquoting one article doesn't change the evidence. Today's warming is unprecedented in speed, rivalling the asteroid event that wiped out the dinosaurs. This is not a "natural fluctuation."

"Carbon levels are only high if you pick your starting point."
Atmospheric CO_2 rose 35 parts per million over 1,000 years after the last ice age. We've done the same in just 14 years — with 8 billion people, not small hunter-gatherer populations.

"The Earth is 20% greener than it was 30 years ago."
True, but mainly due to human interventions: tree-planting programs in China and agricultural practices in India. It does not offset losses in biodiversity-rich regions like the Amazon and Indonesia. Gains exist, but so do massive losses.

"Developing countries need fossil fuels to grow."
Many are leapfrogging directly to clean, decentralised energy systems. This is not charity — it's smart economics that creates jobs, lowers energy costs, and improves health. Energy access and climate action can coexist.

"Our country's emissions are too small to make a difference"
As Dr Rod Carr (former Chair of New Zealand's Climate Change Commission) puts it, *"Humanity is going to have to get rid of that argument, because there are over 100 countries that could use it."* A tonne of CO_2 has the same effect on the atmosphere no matter where it's emitted, and one tonne avoided delivers the same benefit. If every "small" country waited for others to act, no one would move. Climate leadership isn't about size; it's about momentum, direction and example.

Once you've waded through the swamp of climate myths —
dodging Facebook scientists, pub experts, and that one uncle
who insists volcanoes are doing all the warming — you're left
with a more helpful question: *why does any of this matter to you
personally?* Because understanding the facts is essential, but
it's your own "why" that actually gets you to do something
about them.

Shifting Cultures

Environmental protection and social justice movements look
different around the world, but they share something
important: they are accelerating.

Across Asia, Africa, Latin America, Europe, and the Pacific, a
new generation of climate-aware workers, organisers, and
entrepreneurs is reshaping industries from energy and
agriculture to finance, construction, and digital technology. In
many places, climate work is not a "trend". It is a necessity,
rooted in cultural appreciation, Indigenous knowledge, and the
lived experience of climate impacts.

Recent global insights point to a few clear patterns.

Sustainability and entrepreneurship are increasingly
intertwined. A growing share of new businesses is being built
specifically to solve environmental and social challenges, from
regenerative farming initiatives to circular design and repair-
based models.

Younger generations increasingly expect ethics from
employers. Many Gen Z and Millennial workers are choosing
where to work based on values, purpose, and climate
alignment, not just salary.

Climate action is becoming inseparable from justice. Movements across the Global South continue to remind the world that climate solutions must address inequality, colonial histories, land rights, and cultural survival, not simply emissions figures.

Indigenous leadership is rising. From Māori and Pasifika guardianship models in Aotearoa to First Nations stewardship in Australia and beyond, Indigenous worldviews are reshaping conversations about land use, biodiversity, and intergenerational responsibility.

In short, climate work is becoming more global, more intersectional, and more rooted in community. It is not just corporate, and it is not just technical.

Start with WHY

"I never wanted to be a businessman. All I wanted to do was build products I believed in and not destroy the world. Somewhere along the way, that became a business model."
— Yvon Chouinard

Yvon Chouinard, who never intended to run a global business, argues that if you want to change society, you can do it through how you work. Patagonia didn't start as an environmental company; it became one through a clear set of values. Most of us have that same opportunity, even if our business cards don't say 'sustainability'.

In his book and TED Talk, Start with Why, Simon Sinek explores the power of understanding and communicating the purpose, or "why," behind what we do. This is crucial, especially in the context of the climate emergency. As individuals, it's essential to find your 'why' in this space—to connect with what matters to you about the climate crisis, whether it's the preservation of biodiversity, protecting future generations, or ensuring a sustainable planet.

Once you understand your connection to the issue, it becomes easier to find work, make choices, and take actions that align with your values and contribute meaningfully to climate solutions. Acknowledging your personal 'why' can help you remain grounded and motivated, especially when faced with overwhelming climate news or challenging decisions; it serves as a compass amid uncertainty and discouragement. This sense of purpose is vital given the rise of climate anxiety, particularly among younger generations, who are increasingly affected by the crisis's emotional burden.

In Japan, there is a word, Ikigai, which describes the reason you get up in the morning — the meeting point between what you love, what you're good at, what the world needs, and what you can be paid for. It's not treated as a career hack or a motivational slogan, but as a guiding philosophy for a meaningful life. In the Ikigai book, García and Miralles show how communities in Okinawa embody this every day: through purpose, connection, intergenerational support, movement, and a deep sense of belonging. When you know your "why", the "how" becomes far less daunting.

Climate work fits naturally into this idea. If you are searching for direction in your career (or trying to understand where your skills could matter most), climate action sits exactly where the Ikigai circles overlap. It matters to the world, it requires a considerable range of talents, it offers meaningful paid work, and it provides a sense of contribution that runs deeper than any job title.

And Japan isn't the only place offering a philosophy worth borrowing. Denmark's hygge centres wellbeing and belonging, a reminder that you cannot do good work in a burned-out life. Indigenous worldviews, including kaitiakitanga in Aotearoa New Zealand, emphasise guardianship, reciprocity, and long-term thinking; principles that sit at the heart of sustainability, long before we ever put a label on it. Bhutan measures Gross National Happiness, prioritising community and natural living systems over economic growth for its own sake.

Taken together, these perspectives underscore a powerful point for anyone entering climate work: purpose is not a luxury. It is often the difference between burning out or staying in the movement. Ikigai asks: "What is the world calling you to do?" Climate action provides one obvious answer.

Climate Anxiety

Climate anxiety (also known as eco-anxiety) is the chronic fear or worry about environmental destruction and the future of the planet. It's becoming increasingly common, particularly among younger generations, as the reality of climate change becomes more visible and urgent.

Recent research shows that climate anxiety among young people is not primarily driven by media exposure, but rather by a deep sense of disappointment and perceived government inaction.

In a global survey, a study of individuals aged 16 to 25 found that many young people experience intense emotions (such as fear, anger, and helplessness) in response to the climate crisis, which is having a tangible impact on their everyday lives.[21] This growing eco-anxiety is closely linked to the belief that governments are failing to take adequate action to address climate change.

Feeling overwhelmed or anxious about the climate crisis is normal. But anxiety doesn't have to paralyse action; it can be the compass that points to your personal 'why.' Understanding your motivations gives your efforts purpose and keeps you grounded.

As Mark Manson argues in 'Everything Is F*cked', hope isn't the absence of problems; it's choosing what to care about in a

---

[21] Young People's Voices on Climate Anxiety, Government Betrayal and Moral Injury - Elizabeth Marks, Caroline Hickman 2021

world that feels overwhelming. Climate work is much the same: meaning comes from commitment, not comfort.

The Role of the Individual

Once you know your why, the next step is to ask how it translates into your daily life, your job, your choices, and your voice on the broader system. This is where the individual's role comes into focus.

For companies, investing in sustainability isn't just about being environmentally friendly, it's about securing the future of our planet and our businesses. By prioritising sustainability in the workplace, we not only reduce our environmental footprint but also foster innovation, attract socially conscious customers, and build resilient, future-proof organisations. Companies can, and are, embracing sustainability as a cornerstone of their culture, ensuring that every decision made today contributes to a healthier, more sustainable future for generations to come.

To every individual, whether you're working in bars or boardrooms: Sustainability isn't a luxury; it's a necessity. Whether you're making decisions at the top of a financial behemoth or serving drinks at a local bar, your actions ripple across the globe. Embracing sustainability isn't just about saving the planet; it's about safeguarding our collective future, ensuring prosperity for generations to come. From reducing waste and energy consumption to championing ethical sourcing, each of us plays a vital role. Let us unite in our commitment to sustainability, recognising that every small step adds up to significant change.

If you care about climate change, activism can be a powerful way to amplify your voice and contribute to the collective effort for change. Activism, especially when done in groups, helps raise awareness, pressure policymakers, and hold corporations accountable for their environmental impact.

Movements such as Extinction Rebellion (XR), Fridays for Future, and others have demonstrated that organised protests, petitions, and campaigns can lead to tangible change, including the UK's declaration of a climate emergency and the adoption of a net-zero target. Activism can also influence public opinion, shift societal norms, and spark broader conversations about sustainability.

Finding a group of like-minded people who share your commitment to climate action is highly beneficial. It provides a sense of community, support, and shared purpose, which can help combat feelings of isolation or helplessness. Working with others strengthens your impact, as collective action is often more effective than individual efforts. Being part of a group also offers opportunities to learn, collaborate on initiatives, and contribute to long-term solutions. In short, activism, especially when undertaken collaboratively, can effect real change and empower individuals to make a significant difference in the fight against climate change.

Never underestimate the value of connection, or the power of feeling part of a collective. In 2018, a small group of Kiwis living in London came together and created Kiwis in Climate to connect people working in climate and sustainability roles overseas. As many members returned home, the network continued to grow. Today it has expanded into a global community that champions climate action, supports evidence-based advocacy, and engages with policy and public debate.

Groups like Kiwis in Climate exist all over the world. They are filled with people who bring professional expertise, lived experience, and a willingness to share time and knowledge in support of others. These communities do more than create space to connect. They help people feel seen, reduce isolation, and provide a place to speak openly with others who understand the work and share similar values.

Just as importantly, they help turn concern into action. Through submissions, open letters, policy engagement, and grassroots organising, these collectives often become quiet engines of change, linking individual motivation to coordinated impact.

In the lead-up to the UK's net-zero target announcement in 2019, environmental activists, particularly Extinction Rebellion and youth climate strikers, played a crucial role in pressing for more decisive climate action. XR's 2019 protests, including mass arrests and blockades in central London, demanded urgent government action on climate change, including a net-zero emissions target by 2025.

At the same time, the Fridays for Future movement, inspired by Greta Thunberg, saw millions of young people worldwide, including tens of thousands in the UK, marching for climate action. These movements generated significant media attention and public debate.

Disclaimer: It's vital to acknowledge your privilege when engaging in activism. Only participate in actions or public demonstrations where you feel safe and capable, as some forms of climate action can carry risks to your well-being. In the

UK, for example, the government passed the Police, Crime,
Sentencing and Courts Act 2022, which criminalised certain
forms of protest and granted the police greater powers to arrest
or detain individuals, including for planning protests.
Additionally, it's crucial to recognise that the risks associated
with activism may disproportionately affect specific
communities. Statistics show that Black people and other
marginalised groups may be at greater risk of police violence or
discrimination during protests compared to White people.
Always consider your personal safety and the potential risks to
others when deciding how to engage in climate action.

In addition to protests, environmental groups such as Friends
of the Earth and Greenpeace engaged in extensive lobbying,
leading the UK Parliament to declare a climate emergency in
May 2019. This declaration, along with growing pressure from
activists, helped set the stage for the UK government's
adoption of the net-zero target in November 2019. While it's
difficult to attribute the policy shift solely to these protests, the
activism was undeniably a key factor in raising awareness and
influencing political decision-making.

As Maggie Nelson explores in On Freedom, real progress
means navigating complexity without waiting for perfect purity.
This lesson applies directly to climate action, where imperfect
attempts still advance progress.

In 2024, a landmark court case in the United States showed
once again how organised, persistent advocacy can move the
dial. A coalition of public-interest groups challenged the
country's most significant public pension funds, arguing that
their continued investment in fossil fuel companies exposed

pension members to substantial financial and climate-related risks.

The courts agreed.

The ruling stated that pension trustees have a legal duty to consider climate risks in their investment strategies and that ignoring these risks could constitute a failure of fiduciary duty. This decision does not instantly transform global financial flows, but it sets a powerful precedent:
Climate risk is a form of financial risk, and institutions can be held accountable.

This is a reminder that activism does not always take the form of street protests. Sometimes it seems like legal action, shareholder pressure, financial scrutiny, or academic research. All of it matters. All of it adds up. And occasionally, it results in system-shifting wins that ripple far beyond the courtroom.

Knowing your influence as a worker or activist is one thing, measuring your impact is another. Let's explore the tools that help you understand where your actions really count.

SECTION B — Personal Impact

We love a good number. A neat little summary of how well we're doing, or how badly.

Enter the personal carbon footprint.

You'll have seen it: a website that asks how often you fly, what you eat, how many kids you have, and whether you drive a diesel van. Then it gives you a number. Usually in tonnes. Often followed by a finger-wagging infographic about how many Earths we'd need if everyone lived like you.

That number might genuinely change how you think about your life. And it might also be one of the biggest distractions in the climate conversation.

Before we get into carbon footprints, let's explore something far meatier...

Small Decisions, Big Systems

If you want a clear example of how individual choices collide with systemic failure, look no further than food.

Household food waste in the UK (and many other countries around the world) is staggering, and frankly, uncomfortable to sit with when you consider the cost-of-living crisis, the rise of food banks, and the inequality wrapped up in who eats and who doesn't. Estimates suggest UK households discard around 4.5 million tonnes of edible food every year. Perfectly good food. Binned.

Some of this *is* on us as consumers. We overbuy. We forget leftovers. We let produce wilt at the back of the fridge. We shop on autopilot. We can and should do better: planning meals, buying less, understanding that "best before" does not mean "inedible after", and treating food with a bit more respect.

Because wasting food isn't just a financial cost. It's an environmental one. Every tomato, loaf, and ready meal has already used land, water, energy, fertiliser, packaging, refrigeration, and transport before it ever reaches your kitchen.

But households are only part of the picture.

Supermarkets and supply chains play a massive role too, and this is where personal agency meets professional influence. Many supermarkets still discard food before its best-before or use-by date due to cosmetic standards, stock rotation practices, or corporate risk aversion. At the same time, food banks are under unprecedented strain. The Trussell Trust distributed almost 3 million emergency food parcels in 2023–24, the highest on record, with many people facing a genuine "heat or eat" decision.

So yes, at home, we can be more thoughtful shoppers.

But if you work in retail, supermarkets, logistics, sourcing, distribution, policy, or procurement, your influence is far larger than your own grocery basket.

You could:

- advocate for improved stock management
- support redistribution partnerships with food banks
- challenge cosmetic standards that bin edible produce
- expand "wonky" ranges or dynamic pricing

- embed food waste targets into procurement policies

This is the heart of it. Your day job often gives you more climate *and* social impact than your personal life ever will.

And that's the lens we need when we talk about carbon footprints.

Your Carbon Footprint

Climate change is now so frequently referenced it risks fading into background noise.

Meanwhile, cities flood, heatwaves intensify, and "once-in-a-century" storms arrive every other Tuesday. We used to call them natural disasters. Soon they'll just be "the weather."

Before talking about individual footprints, it helps to acknowledge the scale. A world warmed by 2°C, our current best-case trajectory, means collapsing ice sheets, widespread water scarcity, more intense heatwaves, and parts of the planet becoming effectively uninhabitable.

And yet, the solution we're often handed is… recycle more and avoid plastic straws.

Thanks, BP.

Yes, the term *personal carbon footprint* was popularised by an oil company PR campaign. The logic was simple: if we're busy worrying about compostable coffee cups, we're less likely to ask why a small number of corporations drive the vast majority of emissions.

But here's the nuance.

Your carbon footprint does matter, just not for the reasons BP would like.

It matters because understanding your footprint is often the gateway to understanding systems, inequality, and ultimately leverage.

Your carbon footprint is the sum of greenhouse gases generated by your lifestyle: how you travel, how your home is heated, what you eat, what you buy, and the energy you use. Put simply, it's how your daily life stacks up in emissions terms.

Calculating it can feel uncomfortable, but it's useful. Not because it will solve climate change, but because it highlights the big levers. For most people, emissions are dominated by transport, housing, energy, food, and consumption.

Long-term data from the World Resources Institute and Our World in Data shows that more than half of all CO_2 emitted since the Industrial Revolution has been released in just the last 30 to 40 years. That's the world we live in: industrial, fossil fuelled, and built for high emissions.

Why Your Country Matters

What many carbon calculators fail to emphasise is this: your footprint is heavily shaped by where you live.

Your country's energy mix, transport infrastructure, housing stock, planning laws, public transport access, climate, and consumption norms all matter.

Before zooming in on your personal footprint, it helps to zoom out and understand the different lenses used to measure national emissions. These are usually framed in two main ways:

1. Total or cumulative emissions: This looks at how much a country has emitted overall, often going back to the Industrial Revolution. Measured this way, a small group of early industrialised nations account for a large share of historic emissions. That scale matters. Carbon dioxide released 50 or 100 years ago is still warming the atmosphere today.

Many developing countries, by contrast, have contributed relatively little historically, even though they are often the most vulnerable to climate impacts.

2. Per capita emissions: This divides a country's emissions by its population and shows, on average, how much each person is responsible for.

A country can have very high total emissions simply because it has a large population. That does not automatically mean its citizens are living high-consumption lifestyles. In some cases, people may be living modest or precarious lives with low per-person emissions, while the national total appears large.

Looking at both measures together gives a fairer picture.

Total emissions show scale and historic responsibility.
Per capita emissions show patterns of lifestyle, infrastructure, and inequality.

Both matter. And both remind us that climate responsibility is not evenly distributed, either between nations or between individuals.

For example:

• Global average territorial emissions sit around 4–5 tonnes CO_2 per person per year.
• In the United States, territorial emissions are closer to 14 tonnes per person.
• In the UK, consumption-based estimates are often around 10 tonnes per person.
• In Aotearoa New Zealand, consumption-based estimates typically fall between 7–10 tonnes per person.
• The poorest half of the global population emits well below 1 tonne CO_2e per person on average.

Exact numbers vary by methodology and year, but the pattern is consistent. Where you live shapes what "normal" emissions look like.

It is also important to consider cumulative emissions, not just what a country emits today. While China currently has the largest annual emissions in absolute terms, the United States remains the largest cumulative emitter in history, responsible for roughly a quarter of all carbon dioxide emitted since the Industrial Revolution. The United Kingdom, despite its smaller size today, was one of the earliest industrialised nations and ranks among the top historical contributors over the past 150 to 170 years.

This matters because carbon dioxide does not disappear after a year or two. A significant share remains in the atmosphere for centuries, meaning warming today is driven by accumulated emissions. From a fairness perspective, understanding who has contributed most over time is just as important as understanding who emits the most right now.

Acknowledging this doesn't remove personal responsibility. It clarifies where leverage lies.

You may not be able to redesign the power grid, but you can make intentional choices within the system you're in:

• drive less, or choose shared or electric transport
• question the necessity of flights
• adopt lower-impact diets where possible
• prioritise repair, resale, and circular options over constant new consumption

Your individual choices will not fix systemic problems on their own.

But they help you see the system, and understand where your influence begins.

What Are We Aiming For?

Climate science suggests that to give humanity a reasonable chance of limiting warming to 1.5–2°C, global average per-capita emissions need to fall to around 2 tonnes of CO_2e per person per year.

Two tonnes.
Per person.
Per year.

If you currently live in a system where 9 or 10 tonnes per person is considered normal, that's a reduction of more than half. A lot more.

That *is* a radical shift. But the point isn't to shrink lives into austerity. It's to redesign the systems we rely on: energy, housing, transport, food, and consumption.

A realistic carbon footprint tells you two things:

1. Where you stand
2. How far the journey needs to go

But the footprint is only the beginning.

Because what matters next isn't just what you emit — it's what you influence.

And that's where we turn to climate shadow and carbon handprint.

Climate Shadow

Your footprint shows what you emit.
Your influence shows what you change.

Jonathan Safran Foer's *We Are the Weather* explores this idea through everyday choices, particularly food, showing how small, repeated decisions, made consistently and at scale, can shift collective outcomes. It's a reminder that personal action is not about purity or perfection, but about recognising where individual behaviour intersects with culture, systems, and social momentum, and choosing to push those forces in a better direction.

This is where the concept of the climate shadow comes in, a term coined by Emma Pattee. Your climate shadow is the larger, often invisible impact of your choices, behaviours, conversations, and work. It's not just what you emit, but what you enable, normalise, support, or shift.

You might drive a petrol or diesel car today, but push your workplace to electrify its fleet.
You might still eat meat, but use your voice to support lower-impact food systems.
You might fly for work, but you can also help redesign your organisation's travel policy, or your job is in international environmental policy.

Every decision, what you buy, where you work, what you support, how you vote, shapes your climate shadow. And often, that shadow can dwarf your personal footprint.

Your climate shadow also includes your money: where you earn it, where you spend it, and where it sleeps at night.
Your KiwiSaver, pension, bank, employer, and investments are all part of your impact. Every dollar is a tiny vote for the kind of world you want.

Here's the uncomfortable part: many people have no idea where their money is actually being invested. Pension schemes and default investment funds frequently hold shares in fossil fuel companies, deforestation-linked supply chains, tobacco firms, and industries that directly undermine public health and environmental stability. How often do we check? And if we did, would we be comfortable knowing our retirement savings might be built on industries that profit from pollution, addiction, or ecosystem destruction?

Research from ISIO highlights that climate change is not just an environmental risk, but a long-term financial and mortality risk for pension holders themselves. Meanwhile, analysis from

Make My Money Matter has shown that UK pension funds alone are linked to billions of pounds of investment tied to global deforestation. In Aotearoa New Zealand, organisations like Mindful Money make it easier to see where KiwiSaver and managed funds invest, giving everyday people visibility and choice over whether their money aligns with their values.

And money is only part of the shadow.

Your vote also casts one. What are the environmental policies and social commitments of the political party you support? Do they prioritise climate action, education, public health, housing, and infrastructure that protects vulnerable communities? These decisions shape national systems for decades, far beyond the impact of individual lifestyle changes.

When you zoom out to see the whole picture, the shadow often outweighs the footprint, because while systems shape us, we also shape systems, if we choose to.

Carbon Handprint

This is the positive side of the equation: the emissions you help avoid through your actions, skills, or the things you create.

If you design something more efficient, that's a handprint.
If you help your workplace switch to clean energy, that's a handprint.
If you persuade your family to try one plant-based meal a week, congratulations, that's a handprint too.

And here's the critical nuance: Most things have both a footprint and a handprint.

- A heat pump has a footprint (manufacturing, logistics, energy demand), but replacing a gas boiler gives it a massive handprint.
- An EV has a footprint, but replacing an ICE (Internal Combustion Engine) car gives it a handprint that grows every kilometre on clean electricity.

The real question is:
Does the handprint outweigh the footprint?

That's where impact lives.

So, what should you do?

Calculate your carbon footprint, yes. It's a valuable reality check. But don't stop there.

Look at your shadow:
How you vote. Where you put your money. Who you work for. What ideas you spread. What systems you influence.

Then grow your handprint:
Support electrification. Make lower-carbon choices in your workplace decisions. Use your skills to drive change in your workplace or community.

Do the imperfect things that push systems in the right direction.

Because perfect people won't solve this crisis.
It will be solved by ordinary, imperfect people — pushing, nudging, influencing, and refusing to pretend that recycling alone will fix it.

And that starts with you.

A quick note on terminology

At this point, it's worth acknowledging that these terms weren't designed together, by one neat authority, in a perfectly logical system.

Carbon footprint, *carbon handprint*, and *climate shadow* are all useful concepts, but they come from different places, are used in different contexts, and sometimes overlap.

In corporate sustainability and reporting, carbon footprint usually refers to a company's Scope 1, 2, and 3 emissions, the greenhouse gases created through operations, energy use, and value chains. Carbon handprint is often used to describe Scope 4 or *avoided emissions*: the positive impact a product, service, or decision enables elsewhere.

For individuals, the framing shifts slightly.
Your carbon footprint helps you understand the emissions tied to your lifestyle and consumption.
Your climate shadow helps you understand something broader: how your choices, influence, work, money, and voice shape systems beyond your personal emissions.

There isn't a single "correct" definition, and there will always be grey areas. That's okay.

The point of this chapter is not to turn you into a carbon accountant or to have you worrying about which metric you should be measuring or reporting against. Each organisation, sector, and role will approach this differently, and that's entirely appropriate.

The real value here is simpler:

- Understanding where emissions come from
- Recognising where influence sits
- Identifying where you can have the greatest positive impact

If the language helps you think more clearly, use it.
If it starts to feel distracting, let it go.

What matters far more than perfect definitions is this:

Are your actions, decisions, and influence pushing systems in a better direction?

That's the question to keep hold of.

The 3 Cs

Cows, Cars, and Coal. Together, the Food, Transport, and Energy sectors account for roughly half of all human-caused greenhouse gas emissions. In simple terms, reducing emissions from livestock, moving away from coal, and changing how we get around could make a huge difference.

It's not easy, but it's also a massive opportunity for innovation, policy, and meaningful career action.

Cows are a surprisingly big part of the problem. Livestock, especially cattle, produce methane, a greenhouse gas far more potent than carbon dioxide over the short term. Agriculture also drives deforestation, soil degradation, and water pollution. Roughly 14% of global greenhouse gas emissions come from livestock, with beef and dairy the largest contributors.

The scale of our livestock system is staggering. Research published in *Proceedings of the National Academy of Sciences* by Bar-On, Phillips and Milo (2018) estimates that livestock account for around 60% of the total biomass of all mammals on Earth. Humans make up about 36%. Wild mammals account for just 4%. In other words, the animals we farm to feed ourselves outweigh all wild mammals many times over.

This is not just a carbon story. It is a biodiversity story. Climate change and ecological loss are intertwined. As George Monbiot argues in *Regenesis*, climate, biodiversity, and food security are not competing priorities; they are symptoms of the same broken system. A just transition is not about choosing between feeding people and protecting nature. It is about redesigning how we produce food so we can do both.

Solutions already exist. Regenerative farming, improved grazing practices, innovative feed additives, and shifting diets toward more plant-based options can reduce emissions while improving soil health, water quality, and long-term resilience.

Transport is another major lever. Cars and road vehicles account for a significant share of global emissions, contributing to the roughly 16% attributed to the transport sector. Cities designed around private vehicles, long commutes, and car dependency lock in high emissions. Electrifying transport, investing in public transit, and designing walkable, bike-friendly communities are powerful interventions.

But transport emissions are not limited to cars. Freight, including heavy road transport, shipping, and rail, underpins global supply chains and remains closely tied to fossil fuels. Aviation, both commercial and private, is one of the fastest-growing sources of emissions. Flying accounts for roughly 2–3% of global CO_2 emissions directly, and more when high-altitude warming effects are included. The way we move people and goods is inseparable from the energy system that powers it.

Then there is coal and energy. Coal remains the largest single source of global CO_2 emissions, primarily for electricity generation. Fossil fuels overall account for roughly three-quarters of global greenhouse gas emissions. The direction of travel is clear: scale renewables, improve building and industrial efficiency, electrify wherever possible, and phase out coal while supporting workers and communities through the transition.

These sectors are deeply connected. Clean electricity powers electric vehicles. Regenerative agriculture reduces pressure on land and inputs. Urban design shapes transport demand. Solving climate change is not just about swapping technologies; it is about redesigning systems.

Food illustrates this perfectly. The world produces enough to feed around 10 billion people, yet millions still go hungry. The problem is not only production, but distribution, waste, and how land is used. Livestock occupy the majority of agricultural land, yet only a small fraction is used to grow crops eaten directly by people. Redirecting some of that land and feed toward human consumption could feed billions more while easing environmental pressure.

Farmers sit at the centre of this conversation. In many countries they are not simply one industry among many; they are cultural anchors and economic backbones. Farming is often tied to land, identity, and generations of family history.

Regenerative practices such as hedgerow planting, crop and livestock rotation, compost use, and carefully managed herd sizes can restore biodiversity, rebuild soils, and improve long-term resilience. Done well, these approaches can also reduce input costs and open access to markets that value ethical and environmentally responsible food.

At the same time, many farmers operate within economic systems that squeeze margins while costs rise. Global commodity markets and large corporates often capture disproportionate value, leaving primary producers exposed to volatility and unfair returns. Any serious climate strategy must acknowledge this reality. A just transition cannot mean asking farmers to absorb the risk while others benefit.

Instead, farmers should be central to shaping the future. Governments can accelerate progress through incentives, research funding, training, and policies that strengthen both ecosystems and farm viability. Around the world, from the United States and France to Aotearoa New Zealand, India, Australia, Costa Rica, and the United Kingdom, regenerative initiatives are proving that environmental outcomes and economic resilience can align.

In Aotearoa, examples such as on-farm solar projects and Mike Casey's fully electrified cherry orchard in Central Otago show what is possible when innovation meets practicality. The future of farming does not have to be about decline. It can be about leadership.

The core message is simple. We already have the knowledge, tools, and innovation to transform cows, cars, and coal. What we need now is coordinated action across governments, businesses, communities, and individuals. Reducing emissions in these sectors is not just about stabilising the climate. It is about building more resilient communities, fairer economic systems, and careers that genuinely matter.

And Then There's the Missing "C"

We've talked about cows, cars, and coal — three of the biggest levers in the climate system. But there's a fourth lever lurking quietly behind all of them.

Cash

As we explored earlier, when it comes to carbon footprint vs. climate shadow, what we do matters—but *what we fund* can matter even more.

Whether we like it or not, money talks. It funds supply chains, shapes innovation, signals demand, influences policy, and ultimately decides whether cows are raised regeneratively or intensively, whether cars run on batteries or petrol, and whether coal is replaced with renewables or left to burn until the last legal day.

Your financial footprint is part of your climate shadow.

That includes:

- Where you work, the sector your skills are powering.
- How your company spends and invests, including procurement and supply chains.
- Who you bank with and where your pension/ retirement plan is invested.
- How you spend and what you reward with your custom.
- And yes, who you vote for, because policy is where public money goes.

You don't have to become an economist or an impact investor to make a difference. You need to understand that *your financial, professional, and political decisions are all climate decisions.*

Not everyone can control methane emissions from a farm, redesign a city's transport network, or shut down a coal plant. But most people can choose where their money sleeps at night, whom their labour supports, and what kind of future their next transaction quietly builds.

And that's why this is the perfect moment to shift from awareness to action.

SECTION C — Beyond the Individual

Carbon Tunnel Vision

When most people think about climate action, the conversation quickly narrows to carbon emissions. While reducing greenhouse gases is critical, focusing solely on carbon can create a form of "tunnel vision" that misses the bigger picture.

Sustainability isn't just about carbon. It's about the interconnected web of environmental, social, and economic factors:

- Health: Air pollution, heat stress, and climate-related disease outbreaks affect millions globally.
- Education: Access to learning opportunities shapes communities' resilience and capacity to act sustainably.
- Biodiversity: Loss of species and ecosystems reduces the planet's ability to regulate climate and provide resources.
- Social Justice: Workers, indigenous communities, and vulnerable populations are often disproportionately affected by environmental degradation.

You cannot address one of these issues in isolation. This is the essence of the Intersectional Environmentalist movement, coined by Leah Thomas: environmentalism must consider social inequities alongside ecological impacts.

We must act urgently on carbon emissions by investing in credible solutions, peer-reviewed processes, and robust scientific validation, while also ensuring that people's rights, livelihoods, and well-being are protected. Climate action without justice is incomplete action.

We spoke earlier about the impacts of plastic companies, which are substantial in their own right. Still, plastic pollution has persistent environmental impacts, as plastics can take 100 to 1,000 years to decompose. Plastic can fragment into smaller pieces, and micro- and even nanoplastics have now been found in every ecosystem on the planet, from the Antarctic tundra to tropical coral reefs. There are far-reaching, interconnected environmental and health impacts associated with the plastics industry's continued role.

But it's important to step back and acknowledge that even the concept of "carbon tunnel vision" is, in many ways, a privilege. For a considerable proportion of the world's population, carbon emissions are not the most immediate problem; survival is. For communities facing food insecurity, unsafe water, heat stress, flooding, crop loss, or forced migration, climate change isn't an abstract parts-per-million conversation; it's a daily negotiation of risk.

In parts of the global South, the most urgent climate priorities are often protecting access to clean water, securing land rights, preserving biodiversity that supports livelihoods, or defending Indigenous cultural continuity. In some places, "climate action" looks like restoring mangroves, safeguarding fisheries, protecting forests from illegal logging, or ensuring homes can withstand cyclones, none of which show up neatly in a carbon spreadsheet.

And for many Indigenous communities, the framing of "sustainability" itself can feel backwards. Their goal isn't to sustain a broken system, but to uphold their whakapapa, protect sacred lands, honour ecological relationships, and ensure their people can continue their way of life. Climate action, in that context, isn't primarily about reducing carbon; it's about maintaining sovereignty, food systems, identity, and connection to whenua.

Carbon matters enormously, but it is not the only lens, nor is it always the most relevant one. For many people around the world, climate action begins long before carbon reduction and continues long after.

Much of the climate conversation focuses on using less: less energy, less material, less travel, less impact, and reduction matters. But as Ezra Klein and Derek Thompson argue in *Abundance* (2025), solving the climate crisis isn't only about cutting back, it's also about *building better*. Their central idea is that many of our most significant problems stem not just from excess, but from scarcity: a shortage of affordable homes, accessible public transport, renewable energy infrastructure, healthy buildings, and efficient systems. In their view, to solve the crises we face, we need the courage to *construct* what the future requires, not only restrict what the past relied on.

That perspective is compelling, especially when considering electrification, the energy transition, and the systems-level changes needed to decarbonise entire sectors. However, it comes with important caveats. Growth without limits is what got us here, and building at pace only works if what we build honours planetary boundaries, protects ecosystems, and serves communities equitably. Increasing capacity is not, by itself, a climate solution, unless it is *low-carbon, regenerative, and just*.

Yes, we need to build heat pump networks, resilient homes, electrified transport, circular manufacturing systems, and strong communities. But we must build with intention and humility. Otherwise, we risk repeating the mistakes of the old system, just with newer technology.

In other words, climate action isn't only about doing less. It's about creating more of what we want to see, without recreating what we need to leave behind.

Which is a helpful reminder as we move into another key concept: that the purpose of climate action isn't simply to limit damage, but to rebuild economies and communities so that people can thrive *within* planetary boundaries. That's the essence of Doughnut Economics, designing growth not above limits or below social foundations, but in the safe and just space between them.

Doughnut Economics

Before diving into career choices and individual impact, it's helpful to understand the broader economic context in which we operate. Our current global economy is largely capitalist, structured for growth, consumption, and profit. While this system has created wealth and innovation, it has also contributed to environmental degradation, social inequity, and unsustainable resource use.

Doughnut Economics, developed by economist Kate Raworth, offers a framework to think differently. Imagine a doughnut:

- The inner ring represents the social foundation: basic human needs such as food, water, health, education, equity, and political voice. Falling below this ring means people are deprived.
- The outer ring represents the ecological ceiling: the planetary boundaries for climate, biodiversity, freshwater, air quality, and other environmental limits. Overshooting this ring causes ecological harm.
- The safe and just space for humanity exists in the doughnut itself, between the social foundation and ecological ceiling.

This model highlights that actual progress isn't just economic growth, it's thriving within planetary limits while ensuring social equity.

As a professional, understanding this context matters: Are you looking for a career path that fits within existing economic structures and helps companies adapt sustainably? Or do you want to pursue a more revolutionary role, one that actively seeks systemic change toward a fairer, greener economy? There is no single "right" answer, but seeing the bigger picture helps you understand where you can apply your energy, skills, and influence most effectively.

Some countries are already reimagining success beyond GDP. Norway, for instance, has managed to decouple economic growth from emissions; growing its economy without increasing greenhouse gas emissions in proportion. Even more interestingly, the Nordic region consistently ranks among the world's happiest: Finland, Denmark, Norway, Sweden, and Iceland all score top-tier in the World Happiness Report.[22]

Why? According to the report, it's not just about wealth, it's about the quality of institutions (low corruption, strong welfare), high social trust, and the freedom to make meaningful life choices. These are precisely the kinds of systemic values that sit in the sweet spot of the "doughnut", between social needs and ecological limits.

Understanding frameworks like Doughnut Economics helps us zoom out to see that real progress sits in that sweet spot where human well-being rises *without* pushing the planet past its limits. And that's not just theory. Countries such as Norway and others in the Nordic region demonstrate what this can look like in practice: strong social systems, high levels of public trust, good governance, and low levels of inequality, all while steadily reducing per-capita emissions and consistently ranking among the happiest places on Earth.

If Doughnut Economics offers a vision of the safe and just operating space for humanity, and a new way we can reimagine and redesign our economic model, the United Nations Sustainable Development Goals (SDGs) provide a global roadmap that helps identify specific goals.

---

[22] WHR 2020: The Nordic Exceptionalism

UN Sustainable Development Goals (SDGs)

The United Nations Sustainable Development Goals (SDGs) were established in 2015 as part of the 2030 Agenda for Sustainable Development. Agreed upon by all 193 UN member states, they constitute a shared global blueprint for addressing the world's most pressing challenges, including poverty and inequality, climate breakdown, biodiversity loss, and economic instability.

There are 17 goals in total, each with detailed targets and indicators, designed to guide governments, businesses, and communities toward a more equitable, resilient, and sustainable world.

While SDG 13 focuses specifically on Climate Action, the SDGs emphasise a crucial point: *climate does not exist in isolation*. Every environmental issue has social and economic dimensions, and every social issue has ecological implications.

Some of the SDGs most connected to climate resilience and workplace action include:
- SDG 3: Good Health and Well-Being
- SDG 4: Quality Education
- SDG 5: Gender Equality
- SDG 6: Clean Water and Sanitation
- SDG 7: Affordable and Clean Energy
- SDG 12: Responsible Consumption and Production
- SDG 13: Climate Action
- SDG 11: Sustainable Cities and Communities
- SDG 17: Partnerships for the Goals

Taken together, the SDGs are a reminder that sustainability isn't just about carbon. It's about people, systems, fairness, and future-proofing society.

One of the strengths of the SDGs is that they apply everywhere. Whether you live in London, Faro, Auckland, or Manila, the SDGs offer a universal language for progress. However, the relevance of each goal can vary significantly depending on your location.

For example:

- SDG 6 (Clean Water and Sanitation) is critical in regions facing water scarcity or pollution.
- SDG 4 (Quality Education) may be the highest-impact pathway in places where access to schooling is uneven.
- SDG 7 (Clean Energy) drives transformation across both highly industrialised nations and rapidly developing economies, but the barriers and solutions differ.

This global–local flexibility is part of the design. The SDGs were designed to be comprehensive enough to guide international cooperation while adaptable enough for individual countries, regions, and businesses to prioritise what matters most in their context.

"Sustainability" is a word that gets used so often that it can lose its meaning. But the SDGs bring the idea back down to earth. Terms like *clean water*, *health*, *education*, *resilient infrastructure*, and *gender equality* are concrete. They describe real-life outcomes people can relate to, things that shape everyday experience.

And that's the real value of the SDGs. They make sustainability less abstract and more human. They remind us that Climate action is about protecting people's health; clean energy is about affordability and security; circular economy strategies are about reducing waste and conserving resources; and gender and social equity are environmental issues because they determine who faces the greatest risks and who has access to opportunities.

Understanding these connections can help guide your decisions at work, whether you're in engineering, finance, design, policy, operations, or leadership. When you view your role through the SDGs, opportunities to contribute multiply, because you're no longer thinking in silos but as part of a larger system moving towards a fairer and more resilient future.

Project Drawdown

The Sustainable Development Goals give us a shared direction for a fairer, more resilient, liveable world. Project Drawdown helps answer the harder question: *what do we actually do next?*

Founded in 2014, Project Drawdown is a research organisation focused on identifying, measuring, and scaling the most effective solutions to reduce greenhouse gas emissions. Rather than debating whether climate action is necessary, Drawdown asks a more practical question: *which actions work, at what scale, and in what contexts?*

Its work spans energy, buildings, transport, food systems, land use, industry, and social systems, using real-world data and peer-reviewed research to assess climate solutions based on impact, feasibility, cost, and co-benefits. The result is a framework that moves climate action out of the abstract and into everyday decision-making.

One of Drawdown's most useful tools is the Drawdown Explorer, a living, searchable database of more than 100 climate solutions, grounded in evidence and updated as the science evolves.

What makes the Explorer especially valuable is that it doesn't present a single "top ten" list. Instead, it categorises solutions based on real-world readiness and impact:

- Highly Recommended: solutions that meet Drawdown's full criteria for meaningful, scalable emissions reduction and are already being deployed at scale.
- Worthwhile: actions that reduce emissions in specific contexts or at smaller scales.
- Keep Watching: promising ideas where technology, cost, or evidence still needs to mature.
- Not Recommended: approaches that currently don't stand up to scientific or practical scrutiny.

This approach shifts the conversation from *what sounds good* to *what actually works*.

Examples of high-impact solutions highlighted by Drawdown include:

- Onshore wind and utility-scale solar: now among the cheapest forms of new electricity generation in many parts of the world, and already displacing fossil fuel power at scale.

- Heat pumps and electrified heating: replacing fossil-fuel heating systems with high-efficiency electric heat pumps is a proven, scalable solution already being deployed globally, cutting building emissions, improving energy efficiency, and reducing reliance on gas as electricity grids continue to decarbonise.[23]
- Reducing food waste and shifting toward plant-rich diets: solutions that cut emissions while improving food security and health outcomes.
- Refrigerant management: better handling and phasedown of polluting gases used in cooling systems. This is one of the single largest climate opportunities available today, with regulatory and industry pathways already underway.
- Protecting and restoring forests and wetlands: nature-based solutions that deliver carbon storage alongside biodiversity, water, and community benefits.

For each solution, the Explorer provides data on emissions impact, timing, costs, co-benefits, and, importantly, where these solutions are already active today. It includes maps showing regions where impact is highest and highlights the policies, industries, and professions involved in making them work.

The message is clear: climate action is not a single breakthrough waiting to happen. It is a portfolio of solutions, already in motion, that succeed when people across society recognise their role in scaling them.

Another important evolution of Drawdown's work has been through Drawdown Labs and its *Climate Solutions at Work*

---

[23] Yes again, I'm talking about heat pumps! Sorry

research. This work explicitly recognises something that sits at the heart of this book: that climate action doesn't live in a single sector, job title, or department. It lives within work.

The Drawdown team show, clearly and convincingly, that people influence climate outcomes most through their professions, through what they design, finance, procure, build, regulate, communicate, teach, and normalise. This framing has since been echoed widely, including in Deloitte's *Every Job Is Now a Climate Job* and Jamie Alexander's TED talk, which reinforces the same message: wherever we work, we shape systems, and systems shape emissions.

That idea didn't just inspire this chapter. It helped shape the title of this book.

This is why Project Drawdown matters so much to this book. It doesn't ask people to become someone else. It asks them to look at the work they already do, and see the leverage that's already there.

Your job is already a climate job.
Drawdown just gives us the evidence to prove it, and the tools to act on it.

Sustainability and ESG

An individual can want to live more sustainably. A business can intend to become more sustainable. But intention only gets you so far. At some point, especially in business, you need something more concrete than good intentions and a recycling bin.

From the era of Corporate Social Responsibility, meet its more structured, slightly more sober successor: ESG; Environmental, Social, Governance. Think of ESG as a tool companies use to demonstrate they are not just talking about sustainability but also measuring it.

Sustainability is the ambition, providing purpose and direction, but ESG is the framework, utilising metrics and disclosures and comparability.

At a high level, ESG covers three areas. Environmental includes things like emissions, energy use, waste, water, and biodiversity. Social looks at labour practices, community impact, health and safety, and inclusion. Governance focuses on top-level decision-making, transparency, incentives, and accountability.

In theory, this allows customers, investors, employees, and regulators to challenge claims and ask a simple question: Where is the evidence? With rising regulatory pressure across New Zealand, Australia, Europe, and Japan, that evidence is increasingly non-negotiable. ESG reporting is no longer just a "nice to have". In many markets, it is becoming a legal requirement.

But ESG has nuance. It is useful, and it has limits.

This is where Tariq Fancy's work, former Chief Investment Officer for Sustainable Investing at BlackRock, is particularly interesting. Fancy draws a clear distinction between two very different ways of thinking about sustainability.

The first is what he calls an "outside in" lens. This is how ESG is most commonly used in financial markets. It focuses on how environmental and social risks affect a company's financial value. Climate change matters here because it creates risks to profits, supply chains, assets, and reputation. This lens is investor-oriented. It asks, "How does the world affect the company?"

The second is an "inside out" lens. This is closer to what most people mean by sustainability. It focuses on how a company affects the world. Its emissions, its labour practices, its products, and its impact on communities and ecosystems. This lens is impact-oriented. It asks, "How does the company affect the world?"

Both lenses are valid. But they are not the same thing.

Fancy's critique is that ESG has often leaned too heavily toward the outside-in view. In doing so, it can create the illusion of progress. Companies are rewarded for identifying risks to themselves, producing polished reports, and demonstrating good governance, even if their real-world impacts are not improving.

In practice, many ESG frameworks still reward disclosure effort rather than environmental or social outcomes. It is entirely possible for a company with rising emissions, or even a fundamentally harmful business model, to score well on ESG ratings if its reporting, policies, and governance structures look robust on paper.

There is a well-known example where a tobacco company ranked near the top of an ESG index, largely due to strong governance and transparent reporting. Technically impressive. Morally questionable. Not exactly the future most people have in mind when they talk about sustainability.

This does not make ESG "bad". It means we need to be clear about what it is and what it is not.

When ESG is treated as the solution, we risk mistaking reporting for progress. When it is treated as a tool, it can be genuinely powerful.

This is where the concept of double materiality becomes important.

Double materiality is an attempt to hold both lenses at once. While it is defined slightly differently across jurisdictions, the core idea is consistent. Companies should assess both how sustainability issues affect their business and how their business affects the world.

In other words, materiality runs in two directions.

The first is financial materiality. How do climate change, biodiversity loss, resource constraints, and social issues create risks or opportunities for the company? This includes physical risks such as floods and heatwaves, transition risks from new policies or technologies, and market risks from shifting customer expectations.

The second is impact materiality. How does the company's activity contribute to emissions, environmental degradation, inequality, or harm? This includes the full value chain, not just what happens within company walls.

Increasingly, international climate and sustainability disclosure regimes are requiring companies to consider both. The EU's CSRD explicitly embeds double materiality. Other markets, including Australia and New Zealand, are moving in the same direction, even if the language differs. The signal is clear:

understanding climate risk without understanding climate impact is no longer enough.

For people working inside organisations, this matters more than it might first appear. ESG frameworks influence what gets measured, funded, discussed at the board level, and rewarded. They shape incentives. They shape careers. They shape decisions that quietly ripple through supply chains and communities.

Used poorly, ESG becomes a box-ticking exercise. Used well, it becomes an accountability mechanism that connects ambition to action.

We'll come back later to communication skills and greenwashing in more detail, but it's worth noting here that robust ESG frameworks and metrics exist for a reason. They allow businesses to disclose, and market, their products and services with credibility. There are far too many products with "eco" or "green" stamped across the front with very little substance behind them. Regulators are increasingly clamping down on vague or misleading environmental claims, issuing fines and tightening guidance, which is good news for those doing the hard work properly.

Organisations like Eco Choice Aotearoa, whose CEO Laura you'll hear from later, are a strong example of how this can be done well. As New Zealand's official ecolabel, Eco Choice certifies products against rigorous life cycle criteria across multiple environmental and social categories, providing independent assurance that claims are backed by evidence rather than marketing spin.

If you have genuinely improved a product or service, you should be able to promote it confidently, but precision matters. "Good for the planet" is vague and walks dangerously close to greenwashing. "Made with 60% recycled content" or "A-rated for energy efficiency" is clear, measurable, and defensible. The rule is simple: measure, disclose, and be specific. Avoid sweeping claims and let the evidence do the talking.

The challenge, and the opportunity, is to push ESG beyond compliance and towards consequence. To use it not just to ask, "Are we exposed?" but also, "What are we responsible for?"

What this means for you

You do not need to become an ESG expert overnight. In many roles, ESG will sit quietly in the background. In others, it is already as important as financial reporting.

And if you are reading this thinking, "I work in a café, a shop, a bar, or a hospital ward, surely this does not apply to me," you are partly right. You are unlikely to be writing ESG reports as a waiter or retail assistant. But ESG still shows up around you. It influences which suppliers your workplace uses, where food is sourced, how waste is handled, how energy is managed, how staff are treated, and what behaviours are rewarded or ignored. You may not see the acronym, but you feel its effects in rosters, budgets, policies, and decisions made far above your pay grade.

If you are earlier in a corporate or office-based career, ESG is likely to shape your work sooner than you expect. You might see it appear in procurement criteria, risk registers, internal dashboards, investor updates, or board papers. You might be asked to help gather data, explain a number, sit in on a meeting, or justify why something costs more upfront. Understanding what ESG is, and what it is not, helps you make sense of those conversations. It gives you language, context, and confidence.

Even if you are not the one building dashboards or presenting audits to the board, ESG literacy helps you navigate how decisions are made. It helps you understand why certain projects get funded and others do not, why sustainability investments are framed as risk management, where your organisation is exposed or ahead, and when a glossy claim does not match reality.

Because sooner or later, ESG will either become part of your role, or shape the environment you are working in.

The regulatory tide has already turned. Climate reporting is now mandatory for large companies in Aotearoa New Zealand and Australia. Europe's CSRD framework goes much further. Japan has aligned with ISSB standards. Across markets, ESG and climate disclosure are becoming structural expectations, not optional extras.

For younger professionals, this matters. The people who understand these frameworks early will be better positioned to ask smarter questions, spot gaps, and influence how organisations respond, even without seniority or formal authority.

So, the question for business is no longer, "Should we report?"

It is, "What kind of company do we want to be, and what real-world impact are we willing to stand behind?"

And for you, wherever you sit, the question becomes simpler and more personal: do you want to understand the system shaping your work, or be surprised by it later?

We see this clearly in companies like Patagonia, as shared in *Let My People Go Surfing*. Their approach to maternity and paternity leave, flexible working, and childcare support did not begin as a branding exercise. It came from leaders listening to staff, valuing their team, and designing policies around real human needs.

The result? Higher retention, stronger employee satisfaction, deeper loyalty, and a brand reputation that money alone cannot buy. What began as a people-centred decision became a commercial advantage. It improved productivity, reduced recruitment costs, strengthened PR, and built customer trust. And yes, it also sits squarely within ESG metrics under the "Social" and "Governance" pillars: parental leave policies, gender equity, employee wellbeing, turnover rates, and workforce engagement scores.

In some countries, generous parental leave is embedded into national policy and feels almost ordinary. The Nordic countries, for example, offer some of the most progressive shared parental leave frameworks in the world. In others, particularly where statutory leave is limited, companies stepping up voluntarily can be transformative. What is considered "standard" in one context can be quietly radical in another.

So when we talk about ESG, this is what it can look like in practice. It is not just emissions dashboards and carbon accounting. It is also paid parental leave and equitable caregiving policies, transparent pay gap reporting, living wage commitments, safe and inclusive workplace culture, flexible work arrangements and staff training and progression pathways.

These are measurable. They appear in ESG disclosures. But more importantly, they shape real lives.

If you are inside an organisation, ESG literacy gives you language to advocate for better conditions. You can point to staff turnover data, gender pay metrics, engagement survey results, or benchmark policies in peer companies and ask, "Why not here?" You can connect employee wellbeing to productivity, brand health, and customer engagement.

Good ESG practice is not about copying Patagonia wholesale. It is about asking: what does "good" look like in this context? What metrics already exist that we can use to improve outcomes for people, not just report on them? And how can workplace policies contribute to wider societal gains, whether that is shared caregiving, reduced inequality, stronger communities, or healthier families?

Sometimes the most powerful ESG shifts are not dramatic climate pledges. They are decisions made in HR meetings, boardrooms, and team discussions that quietly reshape what work feels like.

And that, too, is climate work.

The Point of Business

At its core, business can be about more than making money. For a long time, success was measured almost entirely by profit. But that view is incomplete. Businesses that last, and that people actually want to work for, tend to balance three interconnected things: people, planet, and profit.

People come first because they are the business. Employees, customers, suppliers, and communities are not "inputs"; they are the system. How an organisation treats people through fair pay, safe conditions, inclusion, flexibility, and respect directly shapes its culture, resilience, and long-term performance. Burn people out, and the business eventually follows.

Planet is no longer optional. Every organisation depends on stable ecosystems, predictable seasons, functioning infrastructure, and access to natural resources. Businesses that ignore their impacts on climate, biodiversity, and materials expose themselves to growing regulatory, financial, and reputational risk, not to mention the physical risks of operating in a warming world. Those that reduce emissions, minimise waste, and innovate responsibly are not just "doing good". They are future-proofing and staying competitive.

Profit still matters. Profit keeps businesses alive. It pays wages, funds innovation, and enables growth. The shift is not about abandoning profit, but about how profit is made. The question is no longer "Are we profitable?" but "Are we profitable in ways that undermine or support the systems we rely on?"

Now, an important reality check.

For many businesses, especially small and medium-sized enterprises, the primary objective is to make money. And that is not inherently wrong. Many SMEs are under real pressure, juggling cash flow, rising costs, and survival. For some, sustainability feels like a luxury they cannot afford.

Again, as we see in *Moral Ambition,* Bregman highlights that there are also thousands, perhaps millions, of very capable, intelligent, well-meaning people working in organisations whose primary purpose is to maximise returns for owners or shareholders. In some cases, that work creates genuine value. In others, it does not. There are entire industries built around extracting value rather than creating it, helping already wealthy people protect assets, exploit loopholes, or shift costs onto others. Not every profitable business benefits society or the environment, and pretending otherwise helps no one.

This is where the question shifts from theory to something more personal.

What does the point of business mean to you?

What kind of organisation do you want to work for? What kind of work do you want to spend your time doing? What does success actually look like in your life? Is it income alone, or is it impact? Is it personal advancement or contribution? Is it helping others, or mainly helping yourself?

There is no single right answer. But there is an honest one.

The Triple Bottom Line, a concept coined by John Elkington in the 1990s, challenged the dominant belief that a company exists solely to maximise shareholder returns. That belief still shapes many business systems today, which is why this shift can feel slow and uncomfortable.

Many directors are bound by fiduciary duties that have historically been interpreted as prioritising short-term financial returns. Even leaders who want to do better often feel constrained by investor expectations, quarterly targets, or outdated governance norms. So when sustainability work feels political, frustrating, or slow, it is not because the logic is flawed. It is because the system was built for a different era.

Understanding this matters.

It helps explain why some organisations resist change, and why others embrace it. It also helps explain why your choices, about where you work, what you support, and how you show up, matter more than they might first appear.

A future-fit business is not one that chooses between profit and purpose. It is one that understands they are linked. Long-term success depends on healthy people and a healthy planet. The organisations that recognise this are already reshaping how decisions are made, what gets measured, and what kinds of careers are possible.

And the people who understand this early, who ask better questions about the point of business itself, will help shape what business becomes next.

That includes you.

Beyond Compliance

Much of the climate conversation focuses on minimum standards, what the law requires. What regulators expect. What is just enough to stay out of trouble? That matters, but it is not the whole story.

Alongside regulation, there is another crucial force shaping change: voluntary standards that deliberately go further than the norm. These frameworks are not about ticking boxes or doing the bare minimum. They exist to redefine what "good" actually looks like, and to pull entire industries forward by proving what is possible.

Three well-known examples are B Corp, Future Fit Business, and the Living Building Challenge.

B Corp is perhaps the most widely recognised. Companies that become Certified B Corporations commit to meeting high standards of social and environmental performance, transparency, and accountability. Certification looks across the whole business, including governance, workers, customers, community, and environment. Importantly, B Corp is not just about having a good product. It asks whether the business model itself creates benefit rather than harm. For many organisations, the real value of B Corp is not the badge, but the discipline it brings. It forces uncomfortable questions, exposes trade-offs, and makes values measurable.

Future Fit Business takes a slightly different approach. Rather than ranking companies against each other, it asks a more fundamental question: Is this business compatible with a thriving future? Its framework is built around science-based thresholds for environmental and social systems, from climate and water to human rights and decent work. The goal is not to be "less bad", but to stop contributing to harm altogether. Future Fit is demanding by design. It makes gaps visible. It shows organisations how far they still have to go and gives them a roadmap to get there.

The International Living Future Institute's Living Building Challenge pushes ambition even further in the built environment. Often described as the world's most rigorous building standard, it sets absolute performance requirements rather than relative improvements. Buildings must generate their own energy, manage their own water, avoid toxic materials, and actively contribute to human and ecological health. There are no easy credits and no partial passes. Either the building performs, or it does not. It exists to show what "best" actually looks like when you remove excuses and focus on outcomes.

But it's only one example.

Across construction globally, organisations such as the World Green Building Council and its national members, including the New Zealand Green Building Council, provide design guides, rating tools, and certification schemes that help benchmark performance and raise ambition. Where building regulations set the minimum standard, these frameworks provide a pathway beyond compliance.

Building codes tell you what you must do. Rating systems and voluntary standards ask what you could do.

Around the world, clients, investors, developers, and asset owners are choosing to go further: lower operational energy, better indoor air quality, reduced embodied carbon, lower water usage, healthier materials, and buildings that genuinely support the people inside them. In many markets, higher performance is no longer niche. It is becoming a signal of quality, risk management, and long-term value.

And this principle is not limited to buildings.

Every sector has its equivalents: industry benchmarks, voluntary standards, disclosure frameworks, certification schemes, performance ratings, and best-practice guides. Some are regulatory. Some are market-driven. Some are grassroots. Together, they create ladders of ambition.

If you care about improving your product, service, or company, start by asking:

What benchmarks exist in my industry?
Who is considered best in class?
What voluntary standards go beyond minimum compliance?
What guidance already exists to help us build better?

You rarely need to invent the pathway from scratch. In most sectors, someone has already mapped the route upward. The question is whether you choose to follow it.

Frameworks like those mentioned are designed to stretch organisations beyond compliance, beyond marketing claims, and beyond incremental change. They give people inside businesses a shared language for ambition, a structure for action, and, often, a reason to push harder than they otherwise could.

Not every organisation will pursue these standards. Many cannot, at least not yet. But they matter because they reset expectations. Today's "above and beyond" often becomes tomorrow's baseline.

For people working inside organisations, these frameworks are helpful even if your employer never formally signs up. They provide reference points. They help you ask better questions. They offer examples of what leadership can look like when values are taken seriously and translated into practice.

They remind us that progress is not only about meeting today's rules but also about shaping tomorrow's norms.

SECTION D — Careers, Jobs, and You

So now you've met ESG: not the most glamorous part of the sustainability conversation, but undeniably influential. It gives businesses a way to measure, report, and be challenged on what they claim to be doing. Important? Absolutely. Exciting? Maybe not. But useful? Very.

Here's the real point. Knowing the frameworks matters, but knowing how to use your role, your skills, and your career to create change, matters more.

Frameworks don't shift the world. People do.

Which brings us neatly to the next section.

How do you take everything you now understand about sustainability, climate impact, careers, and influence and actually turn it into action?

The Rise of Green-Collar Jobs

As we move from your personal journey, your why, your climate anxiety, and the scale of your carbon footprint, we arrive at one of the most hopeful parts of this story: work. Not just any work, but green-collar work. The kind that lets you make a living *and* a difference.

Green-collar roles are no longer the niche endpoint of sustainability conversations; they're increasingly a core part of the global labour market. LinkedIn's Global Green Skills Report

2023 found that job postings requiring at least one green skill increased by 22.4% in a single year, while the share of workers with green skills only grew by 12.3%. In short, the world is asking for help faster than we're training people to deliver it.

And these aren't just roles on wind farms or solar installations. LinkedIn now categorises green skills across areas like pollution reduction, sustainability reporting, supply chain reform, engineering, finance, construction, manufacturing, energy optimisation, and urban planning. If an industry interacts with the planet (which is all of them), it now increasingly has roles where climate impact matters.

Global analyses suggest that the transition to a low-carbon economy could significantly reshape labour markets. The International Energy Agency estimates up to 14 million new jobs could be created globally by 2030 under its Net Zero scenario. Meanwhile, a joint World Economic Forum and McKinsey study projects that approximately 14.4 million roles will be affected by the transition by 2030, with a net gain of around 9.6 million jobs once shifts in high-emission sectors are accounted for. These figures rely on meaningful policy action, but they demonstrate that the movement is underway.

Here in Aotearoa New Zealand, the organisation Rewiring Aotearoa has shown we've reached an "electrification tipping point".[24] Household energy costs have risen sharply, so switching from fossil-fuel heating to efficient electric systems, such as heat pumps, and installing rooftop solar can deliver

---

[24] Rewiring Aotearoa is an independent, non-partisan, non-profit. It is a registered charity that researches energy, climate, and electrification, advocates for these priorities, and supports communities through the energy transition.

immediate savings. What was once a purely ethical decision is increasingly becoming the obvious financial one. And when sustainability starts making sense to your accountant, you know momentum is shifting.

This reflects a much broader global trend: the energy sector is undergoing one of the most profound transformations in modern industrial history. A striking example is Ørsted, the Danish energy company formerly known as *DONG Energy* (Danish Oil and Natural Gas). In less than two decades, Ørsted shifted its business model from fossil fuels to becoming one of the world's largest offshore wind developers. They didn't just "go green"; they replaced declining fossil revenue with one of the fastest growing, most resilient energy businesses on the planet. Their story is a reminder that entire industries *can* pivot and thrive in a decarbonising world.

And this isn't only about innovation; it's also about justice

The concept of a just transition argues that workers in high-emission industries should be supported, upskilled, and moved into emerging sectors rather than left behind. Winning on climate but losing on fairness isn't a win. 'Just Transition' is a recurring theme throughout this book, as we've already discussed in relation to the role of farmers.

But here's the real heart of this: your influence doesn't depend on having 'sustainability' in your job title.

Supply chain managers, for example, often make decisions that determine 80–90% of a company's environmental impact.[25]. Every supplier selected, every material chosen, and every

---

[25] PwC articles – your suppliers' ESG profile counts.

logistics route approved has implications for emissions, waste, and resource use. And yet most procurement decisions are still analysed through the same familiar lens: Cost, Time, Quality.

We need to expand that lens.
Carbon (and broader environmental metrics) must sit alongside them.
The truth is: many professionals already hold quiet power over their organisations' sustainability outcomes. They haven't yet been supported or encouraged to use it.

You don't need to wait for a radical career change to make a difference. You can pivot into a specialist climate role if that excites you — or stay where you are and apply a sustainability lens from within. The point isn't whether your job title sounds "green." It's whether your work helps build a future that continues to function.

People are already making that move. Some are posting "I quit" on LinkedIn and retraining entirely. Others are staying put and getting strategic: influencing procurement, redesigning workflows, challenging outdated targets, prioritising new suppliers, or simply asking questions that no one else has yet.

Because decarbonisation isn't just about changing the world. It's about changing how the world works.

Whether you install heat pumps, manage supply chains, lead finances, design infrastructure, or make executive decisions, the climate economy is arriving. And it's hiring.

The question is no longer "Is this coming?"
It's "Are you ready to move with it?"

Dark Green Vs Light Green Jobs

As we've already seen, green-collar jobs are on the rise, and not just in places with rooftop turbines or "eco" in the company name. Climate roles are showing up everywhere. But if we assume the only way to make a difference is to become a sustainability consultant or join a solar startup, we miss a much bigger opportunity.

Climate action isn't only about changing industries; it's about changing how you work within them.

If you already enjoy your career, you might not need to abandon it and start over. You can stay where you are, learn new skills, and apply a sustainability lens to your work. Alternatively, if you're starting out or ready for a central pivot, you may choose to join an organisation where environmental impact is core from day one.

These two approaches are often described as Light Green and Dark Green roles.

- Dark Green Jobs are dedicated entirely to environmental outcomes — renewable energy engineers, biodiversity specialists, sustainability strategists, circular-economy designers. These roles sit within organisations whose mission is inherently climate-positive.
- Light Green Jobs exist in every sector, even those not traditionally viewed as "green." This could be a product designer embedding circular principles, an operations manager reducing waste, a procurement lead shifting suppliers, or an engineer choosing lower-carbon materials.

You don't change your profession, you change how you practise it.

And here's something important: Many companies don't have *any* green roles yet- and that's often where the work begins.

You may be the first person to raise sustainability in a meeting. The first to ask a question about carbon in a purchasing decision. The first to suggest including climate considerations in a product design review. No job title required.

Later in the book, in *Change Jobs or Change the System*, we explore how to understand your agency within your existing role:
How much influence do you have? How can you use it? Can you help your company define the roles and responsibilities that don't yet exist? Could you advocate for integrating carbon into procurement metrics or building environmental awareness into everyday decisions?

In truth, transforming the job you already have can sometimes have a greater impact than switching industries entirely. You're influencing decisions that already affect emissions. You're shifting systems from the inside. You're showing colleagues what's possible in environments they understand and trust.

It might not come with a flashy new job title, but the ripple effect can be far greater.

Climate Action Example – The Role of the Engineer

Engineering New Zealand gives a strong example of how professionals can lead from within. In their Climate Action guidance, they note:

"Climate action is taking intentional steps to mitigate and address the reasonably foreseeable impacts of climate change... The solutions require rethinking accepted ways of operating... and gaining new competencies... The solutions require individual engineers to adapt their practice to a changing world."

Some engineering jobs are already Dark Green, such as work in renewables or environmental design. However, many engineers work in sectors that aren't traditionally considered climate-focused. That's where Light Green potential is often most powerful. Making a better material choice, rethinking a design, upgrading a process, that's how sustainability starts to embed itself where it didn't exist before.

The first step is identifying where your work intersects with environmental impact. The second is choosing to act on it.

Some of the most influential climate leaders in the UK construction sector haven't come from people with "sustainability" in their job titles; they've come from engineers quietly asking better questions about their own disciplines.

In particular, structural engineers have increasingly found themselves at the forefront of climate action. This isn't accidental. Structural elements—concrete, steel, foundations, and frames—often account for the largest share of a building's embodied carbon. Long before carbon became a mainstream topic, many engineers were already grappling with material efficiency, optimisation, and whole-life performance. Carbon gave language and urgency to work that was already underway.

Two individuals in the UK who exemplify this shift are Will Arnold and Clara Bagenal-George.

Will Arnold is a structural engineer who has been a leading advocate for embedding embodied carbon limits into building regulations. He is one of the founders of Part Z, a proposed amendment to the UK Building Regulations that would introduce mandatory whole-life carbon assessments and carbon limits for new buildings.

Part Z is intentionally practical. It does not require new technologies or radical design approaches; instead, it seeks to make carbon a regulated design parameter, much like fire safety or structural integrity. Under Part Z, developers would be required to measure, report, and ultimately reduce the whole-life carbon impacts of buildings, shifting carbon from a voluntary consideration to a minimum standard.

What makes Part Z powerful is not just the policy proposal itself, but also the way it was developed: openly, collaboratively, and with input from engineers, architects, consultants, academics, and policymakers. Will's role has been one of translation and persistence, helping turn technical understanding into something legible and actionable for the government.

Clara Bagenal-George represents a similar form of leadership. She is a building performance and sustainability specialist and has played a central role in the Low Energy Transformation Initiative (LETI).

LETI began as the London Energy Transformation Initiative, a volunteer-led network of built environment professionals sharing knowledge on low-energy design. As its influence expanded beyond London, it became the Low Energy Transformation Initiative, reflecting both its success and its national relevance.

LETI has produced some of the most widely cited guidance in the UK construction sector, covering operational energy use, embodied carbon, building performance gaps, and net-zero pathways. Crucially, its work is evidence-based, open-source, and practitioner-led, designed to support professionals who want to go beyond minimum compliance and design buildings that genuinely perform.

In recognition of her contribution to sustainable construction and industry leadership, Clara was awarded an MBE in the King's 2024 Birthday Honours.

It's important to say this clearly: neither Part Z nor LETI are the product of a single individual. Their success comes from collective effort, working groups, peer review, consultation, disagreement, iteration, and trust. Will Arnold and Clara Bagenal-George are effective not because they act alone, but because they are credible, collaborative, passionate, and deeply respected by their peers.

Their work also aligns closely with other UK initiatives, including the UK Net Zero Carbon Buildings Standard, demonstrating that progress accelerates when guidance, regulation, and professional culture reinforce one another.

Both examples show that climate leadership often starts by examining your existing role and asking, "What more could this be?"

Neither Will nor Clara waited for permission. Neither stepped outside their profession; they expanded it. They saw that building regulations set minimum expectations, not best practice. And they chose to help raise the floor.

This is climate action in practice. Not protest or perfection, but professionals recognising their leverage, their expertise, and their responsibility, and choosing to use it.

Your job is already a climate job. The question is how far you decide to take it.

Climate Action Example – Supermarket Workers

Whether you're stacking shelves at 6am, working the checkout on a late shift, driving delivery vans across town, fixing refrigeration units, managing inventory, negotiating supplier contracts, designing marketing campaigns, or sitting in head office reviewing margins; your job sits right at the heart of one of the biggest climate contradictions of our time.

Supermarkets are where abundance and scarcity collide.

Across the world, supermarket workers are often paid minimum or near-minimum wages. Many are under pressure just to make rent or cover groceries. And yet, every day, they see enormous amounts of perfectly edible food thrown away because of "best before" dates, cosmetic standards, bulk promotions, forecasting errors, over-ordering, rigid stock rules, or the pressure to keep shelves looking permanently full.

If that feels uncomfortable, that's because it is.

This isn't a criticism of supermarket workers. It reflects a system that asks people to participate in wasteful practices while often giving them very little power to change them.

But power and responsibility show up differently depending on where you sit.

If you're on the shop floor, you may not control procurement or pricing, but you see patterns. You know which products are constantly over-ordered. You see what gets reduced and what gets binned. Your lived experience is data. Asking questions, flagging recurring waste issues, supporting food-rescue partnerships, or even starting informal conversations about improvements are small but meaningful acts.

If you're a supervisor or floor manager, your influence grows. You may shape ordering decisions, markdown timing, staff training, storage practices, and how rigidly certain rules are applied. You can evaluate earlier discounting, support redistribution partnerships, and challenge the assumption that "full shelves at all times" equals success.

If you're a delivery driver or logistics planner, you influence route efficiency, fuel use, packaging returns, and spoilage rates. If you work in maintenance, refrigeration, or facilities, you shape energy use, refrigerant management, and equipment performance. If you're in procurement or head office, your leverage is even greater; supplier contracts, forecasting algorithms, promotions, packaging decisions, and performance metrics shape waste long before food reaches a shelf.

There are multiple pressure points.

And yes, grassroots action is possible. Many meaningful shifts inside large organisations have started with informal "green teams" or small working groups. If you're genuinely passionate, you may find colleagues who feel the same. Together, you can approach management with constructive proposals, pilot ideas, or evidence from other retailers doing better.

But here's the important nuance.

This is not your sole responsibility. And it is not your obligation to fix systemic failures in your unpaid spare time.

Before taking on additional work, consider:

- Do you realistically have capacity alongside your existing workload?
- Are you being asked to do emotional or strategic labour without recognition or pay?
- Do you have at least some manager or senior-level support?
- How hierarchical is your organisation, and how open is it to bottom-up ideas?

Change without top-down backing is often slow and exhausting. In highly rigid or hierarchical companies, informal efforts can stall without senior sponsorship. We explore more in Part 2 how to assess your organisation's culture, map influence, and navigate these dynamics carefully.

None of this is about guilt.

It's about recognising that if you work in a supermarket, at any level, you are already positioned within one of the most powerful leverage points in the global food system.

Your job is already a climate job.

The real questions are:
How much room do you have to push?
Who can you push with?
And how do you protect your own wellbeing while doing it?

Climate Action Example – The Role of the Banker

If engineers shape the physical world, finance shapes the conditions under which that world is built.

Banks, investors, insurers, fund managers, and grantmakers sit upstream of almost every climate outcome. What gets funded, insured, priced, or excluded determines what is possible long before a shovel hits the ground. This is why international climate frameworks consistently identify finance as a central lever for climate action.

The United Nations Framework Convention on Climate Change (UNFCCC) defines climate finance as funding that supports mitigation and adaptation actions to address climate change, flowing from public, private, and alternative sources at local, national, and international levels.[26] In practice, this includes everything from large-scale infrastructure investment to concessional loans, grants, guarantees, and risk-sharing mechanisms. Climate finance is not a niche activity; it is about aligning capital with long-term planning and emissions reduction across the entire economy.

Some finance roles are already "Dark Green". These include work in climate funds, impact investing, green bonds, and development finance institutions that focus explicitly on mitigation and adaptation. But, as with engineering, the most powerful influence often sits in "Light Green" roles:

---

[26] UNFCCC, *Introduction to Climate Finance*

mainstream banking, corporate finance, credit, insurance, treasury, and investment analysis.

This is where finance professionals quietly decide what is normal.

A lending decision that favours energy-efficient buildings.
A risk model that accounts for climate exposure.
A cost of capital that reflects transition risk.

These are not radical acts. They are incremental, professional decisions that, over time, reshape markets.

In Aotearoa New Zealand, this logic is already visible. Firms like Pathfinder Asset Management have built entire investment strategies around ethical and sustainable investing, integrating environmental, social, and governance considerations into portfolio construction and actively excluding fossil fuels and harmful industries. Pathfinder has also become the first KiwiSaver provider to achieve B Corp certification, signalling that financial performance and positive impact are not mutually exclusive. Their model demonstrates that climate-conscious finance is not theoretical; it is commercially viable and increasingly mainstream.

At the public level, climate finance is also embedded in international development and foreign policy. Through the Ministry of Foreign Affairs and Trade, New Zealand supports climate action across the Pacific and beyond, funding adaptation, resilience, and low-emissions development in countries least responsible for climate change but most exposed to its impacts.[27] This work recognises that finance is not neutral: how and where money flows reflects values, power, and responsibility.

At the organisational level, Project Drawdown's Job Function Action Guides for finance and grantmaking provide a practical lens for individual professionals. They outline how people working in finance can integrate climate considerations into everyday responsibilities: adjusting investment criteria, questioning assumptions about growth and risk, engaging clients on transition plans, and supporting projects that reduce emissions or build adaptive capacity.[28] For grantmakers, this includes funding systems change, capacity building, and long-term outcomes rather than short-term outputs.

What's striking is that none of this requires abandoning financial discipline. In fact, climate-aware finance is increasingly aligned with good risk management. Climate change introduces material financial risks: physical damage, supply chain disruption, asset stranding, regulatory change, and social instability. Ignoring these risks is not neutral; it is a choice to misprice the future.

Many influential climate leaders in finance did not set out to "work in climate". They were bankers, analysts, advisors, or fund managers who began asking better questions within their existing roles. What assumptions sit behind this return? What

---

[27] MFAT, *Climate Change Support*

[28] Project Drawdown, *Finance* and *Grantmaking Action Guides*

happens if this asset becomes stranded? Who bears the downside risk? Who benefits?

Over time, those questions compound.

As with engineering, finance leadership is rarely individual or heroic. It is collective, institutional, and iterative. It happens through committees, credit policies, investment mandates, reporting frameworks, and quiet persistence. It is about shifting climate from a reputational issue or CSR add-on into a core consideration of value, risk, and responsibility.

This is climate action in practice. Not protest or perfection, but professionals recognising where leverage sits and choosing to use it.

Your job is already a climate job.
The question is how consciously you choose to finance the future.

Economic Opportunity

Understanding how your role can change the system naturally leads to the broader picture: the economy itself.

Climate action isn't just necessary, it's increasingly *profitable*. The green collar boom isn't just a moral movement; it's becoming an economic one. Job demand is outpacing the supply of green-skilled professionals; governments are investing in upskilling; and entire sectors are redefining what constitutes "good business."

Today, whether you work in finance, logistics, design, engineering, marketing, or IT, climate impact is increasingly part of your job, whether you asked for it or not. What used to be "nice to have" is quickly becoming essential.

The Rise of Sustainability Professionals

The acceleration is apparent. Businesses, governments, and non-profits now recognise that responding to climate change, managing ESG risk, and tracking progress toward net zero is no longer optional; it's expected. Yet many organisations are still struggling to determine *how*, which is why demand for sustainability capability is outpacing supply.

Some roles are explicitly climate-focused, such as sustainability consultants, carbon analysts, and renewable energy engineers. Others emerge within existing operations, product teams, supply chain functions, or strategy departments. A 2020 survey found that 63% of UK employees want to develop sustainability-related skills to become more valuable, partly out of purpose, partly out of pragmatism.

Companies that ignore sustainability risk reputational damage, regulatory exposure, and talent loss. Those that embrace it benefit from efficiency gains, investor support, customer trust, and the ability to attract and retain people who want meaning in their work.

Sustainability is no longer a department. It's a business-critical capability.

Whether in Dark Green roles or Light Green ones, your career can be a lever for change, not just for your own footprint, but for the systems and people you influence.

Because right now, the job market isn't just looking for professionals.
It's looking for people who can turn ambition into action.

And that, conveniently, is where you come in.

Climate Comms

If you ever needed proof that bad storytelling can delay climate progress, look no further than the UK's relationship with heat pumps. These systems have been used successfully for generations across Europe, Asia, and the US. And yet, the public has been told (loudly and persistently) that "heat pumps don't work." Not because of performance issues. Because of perception issues.

Years of negative coverage, amplified by stakeholders invested in maintaining fossil-fuel heating, shaped public opinion long before most people had ever seen a heat pump. Say something loud enough, for long enough, and it becomes "common sense." This isn't a story about heat pumps. It's a story about storytelling, and what happens when we get it wrong.

And that's why good storytelling matters. Facts inform. Stories move.

Richard Powers' *The Overstory* (a modern classic of eco-fiction) shows this beautifully. In it, forests and trees aren't just environmental features; they are characters with histories, relationships and agency. Readers come away not with data on biodiversity loss, but with a felt understanding of interconnection. That emotional shift, seeing nature as something we belong to, not something we use, is often the missing ingredient in climate communication. In other words, sometimes a novel can change how someone sees a tree in a way a thousand-slide presentation never will.

And this goes far beyond novels. Creatives — writers, artists, comedians, filmmakers, designers, musicians, advertisers, and storytellers of every kind — play a profound role in shaping public sentiment toward climate action. Think of Sir David Attenborough, whose voice has quietly educated, soothed and inspired generations. His documentaries have brought the natural world and its decline into millions of living rooms. He never shouts. He never lectures. And yet he may have done more to shape the UK public's environmental consciousness than any policy paper ever could. That is the power of story.

A powerful example of humour meeting climate communication comes from Climate Science Breakthrough's "Climate Science Translated" series, which pairs scientists with performers to make complex science more relatable. In the UK, comedians such as Jo Brand, Nish Kumar, Kiri Pritchard-McLean, and the satirical character Jonathan Pie have helped translate dense climate messages into language that feels immediate and human. Their work has been viewed by millions and featured in mainstream media, showing that when comic timing meets climate data, familiar voices can reach beyond the usual audiences while keeping the science intact. More recently, Emmy-winning comedian David Cross teamed up with climate scientist Michael Oppenheimer to apply a blend of sharp wit and direct messaging to climate realities, further illustrating that humour isn't frivolous — it's a tool for connection and influence.

It appears everywhere: in the humour of climate comedians like Stuart Goldsmith and Matt Winning; in the striking murals of artists like Banksy; in the visual worlds created by filmmakers like Hayao Miyazaki. Even brand advertising, when done well, can help normalise climate solutions, from electric vehicles to heat pumps to plant-based food, simply by making them feel familiar rather than futuristic.

These are the cultural touchpoints that shift attitudes long before policy does. And with marketing now one of the fastest-growing, best-paid creative professions, there's a genuine question worth asking: *What are you choosing to amplify?* Are you using your talent to sell products that add little value to people's lives or actively harm the planet, or are you using those same skills to tell stories of justice, repair, possibility and a future worth building? Creativity isn't just entertainment. It's agency.

Which brings us to three critical lessons:

1. Communication is a climate tool.
The best engineers can design the most innovative systems, but if public perception is shaped against them, nothing will scale. We need as many communicators, marketers, educators and storytellers in this space as we do designers, scientists and policymakers. (Eco-fiction reminds us why it matters; we need both the blueprint and the story).

2. The problem isn't only greenwashing. It's also greenhushing.
Some organisations exaggerate their sustainability performance (greenwashing). Others stay silent for fear of being criticised (greenhushing). Both delay progress. Honest, confident storytelling is essential if we're to shift culture.

3. Credible, relatable and emotionally compelling stories create change.
You don't have to be an engineer to drive climate action; you could be the person who frames the work, so it gets funded, trusted and adopted. Because sometimes the difference between "It doesn't work" and "It's the better choice" is how it's explained.

And sometimes the difference between concern and commitment lies in how the story is told.

Speaking with Graham Hendra (Featured in Part 3), he suggested reading James Delingpole's *Watermelons* (*How Environmentalists are Killing the Planet, Destroying the Economy and Stealing your Children's Future*), which shows us that climate change is not debated on evidence alone. For many, it has become a proxy for deeper political and cultural anxieties, which helps explain why facts alone rarely change minds.

Translating Sustainability into Your Career

Understanding the environmental and social crises is only the first step. The real turning point is when you begin asking: *"What can I do in my work that genuinely makes a difference?"* Knowing is essential, but doing is transformative.

Carbon tunnel vision reminds us that sustainability isn't just about emissions. It touches health, education, biodiversity, housing, energy affordability, justice, and wellbeing. Seeing this interconnectedness helps you understand where your skills and influence can have the greatest impact, not just in tackling CO_2, but in creating meaningful change across systems.

The UN Sustainable Development Goals (SDGs) provide a functional compass. Whether you're working in engineering, finance, operations, or communications, your choices can contribute to multiple outcomes. Designing low-carbon systems supports climate action. Selecting ethical suppliers improves working conditions and drives responsible production. Advocating for diversity or workplace well-being promotes social equity. Your job doesn't have to be titled "sustainability" to contribute to it.

This is where ESG frameworks can help. While sustainability speaks to purpose, ESG translates that purpose into measurable action. By understanding how environmental, social and governance criteria shape decision-making, you can identify where your organisation has impact, help track improvements in operations or supply chains, and make better-informed choices that align business value with societal value.

So where does this leave you? There are roles fully dedicated to sustainability (*dark-green roles*) where your day-to-day work explicitly focuses on climate or social outcomes. But there are also *light-green roles*, roles within existing teams or industries where you can shape how things are done. That might look like an engineer optimising a product's efficiency, a designer embedding circularity, or a marketer helping communicate honest progress. The question isn't whether your work *can* make a difference, but *how*.

Ultimately, it comes down to agency. Do you want to work within current systems to improve them incrementally? Or do you want to help challenge and redesign them? Both paths matter. Your career can be a lever for change. Every decision you make, about projects, suppliers, materials, design, and messaging, can either reinforce the status quo or help build a regenerative, equitable future. The first step is awareness. The next is intentional action, right where you are.

Closing Part 1: The Basics

If you take anything from this first section, I hope it's that the climate crisis is not a single issue, but a convergence of many: environmental breakdown, social inequality, economic instability, technological disruption, and shifting expectations of what work should be.

We've explored the science and the urgency, the poly-crisis and its cascading impacts, and we've challenged the idea that climate action is only about reducing emissions. It's about rethinking systems—energy, housing, transport, supply chains, business models—and recognising the transition ahead as both a risk and a once-in-a-generation opportunity.

The truth is, there is no neutral ground anymore. Every job, every project, every investment choice either reinforces the current trajectory or helps shift us toward a more resilient, equitable, and regenerative future. The question is no longer *"Does my work affect climate change?"*, but *"How can I use my work to influence what happens next?"*

Which brings us to **Part 2: The Work**. Because understanding the crisis is essential, but understanding your place within it is where change begins. This next section is an invitation to identify where your career, influence, and voice fit within the transition already underway.

Knowledge helps us see what's at stake. Work is where we start shaping what comes next.

PART 2: The Work

Part 1 focused on understanding the climate crisis: the science, the scale, and the role individuals and organisations play within it.

Part 2 is about what comes next.

Because once you understand something, you have to decide what to do with it.

After reading Part 1, there are four paths in front of you.

The first is to do nothing. Close the book. Put your head in the sand. Carry on as if none of this is real, none of it is urgent, and none of it will touch your life. This is an option. It is also, I suspect, an unlikely one for anyone who has actively bought this book, chosen to read it, and made it this far. Still, it is worth noting, because many people end up here by default. Not because they are bad people, but because the scale of the problem can feel overwhelming, and avoidance is a very human response.

If you choose any of the other three paths, you are choosing some version of action. Action does not have to be dramatic. It does not have to be perfect. It just has to be real.

Here are the other three ways people tend to create impact over time.

Path 1: Start where you are.
Use your current role, workplace, community, or sphere of influence to make more informed, future-ready decisions. This might involve questioning outdated practices, improving how work is done, reframing business cases, or helping your organisation adapt to what is coming.

Path 2: Build climate and sustainability into your skillset.
Develop the knowledge and capabilities to influence change more directly. For some people, this becomes a formal sustainability role. For others, it means adding climate literacy,

systems thinking, and communication skills to an existing profession.

Path 3: Change roles, organisations, or sectors.
Some people pivot fully, moving into solution-focused industries. This can be energising and meaningful, but it comes with trade-offs: uncertainty, retraining, and sometimes starting again from a different rung on the ladder.

None of these paths is better than the others. All are needed. Most people will move between them over time, and many will blend them. You might start by changing habits at home, then build skills, then influence your workplace, then eventually shift roles. Or you might do the opposite. The point is not to follow a strict recipe. The point is to do what works for you.

You do not need to read this part as a checklist. Think of it as a map. You may take different routes at different times, and some paths will matter more depending on your role, experience, personality, energy, and circumstances.

Who This Section Is For, and Why That Matters

Part 2 focuses mainly, though not exclusively, on the commercial and private sector. That is where many people spend their working lives, and where enormous influence sits. Businesses shape supply chains, product design, financial flows, employment patterns, and public narratives. When commercial workers shift, industries shift.

But climate and social impact work extends far beyond boardrooms.

As Baina Ubushieva discusses in their UNDP study paper[29], it includes teachers supporting the next generation; social workers caring for vulnerable families; healthcare workers saving lives in increasingly unstable conditions; conservationists protecting ecosystems; community organisers building local capabilities; charity workers safeguarding turtles in Nicaragua, kākāpō in Aotearoa, or restoring wetlands closer to home; comedians using humour to engage people on complex topics; artists and filmmakers helping audiences feel what data alone cannot; and frontline public-sector staff delivering essential services under immense pressure.

Many of these people are already overworked, underfunded, and close to burnout. Their contribution to a thriving, equitable future is enormous.

This book is not asking everyone to suddenly do more.

It is recognising that many already are doing more, often with less support than they deserve.

Instead, the aim here is to inspire, encourage, and equip those who want to use their existing roles, particularly in the private sector, as levers for positive change. Not by working harder, but by working differently. More consciously. More strategically. With a clearer understanding of the systems we are all operating within.

Wherever you sit, in an office, on a construction site, behind a till, in a classroom, a hospital, a server room, a studio, or at a kitchen table, you have a role to play.

Part 2 is about helping you understand what that role could look like, and how to make it work in practice.

---

[29] At the Nexus of Human Rights and Climate Change: A Rights-Based Approach to Environmental Impacts and Policy Responses, UNDP, 2023

Experience, Privilege, and Reality

Everything in this section comes from lived experience: mine and the many people I have spoken with while writing this book. But your path may look very different from mine, and that matters.

People enter climate and sustainability work from wildly different starting points. Some have supportive employers; others do not. Some have financial or educational security; others face systemic barriers every day. Culture, identity, safety, confidence, neurodiversity, health, caring responsibilities, and opportunity all shape how easily someone can speak up, push for change, or take career risks.

What works for one person will not automatically work for another.

So, as you read this, take what helps and leave what does not.

Be flexible. Be patient. Be kind to others, and to yourself.

And above all, be mindful of the system you are operating in. Seek support wherever you can. Find allies. Build connections. This work is hard enough without trying to do it alone.

From Awareness to Action

Before we get into tactics, tools, and frameworks, there is one idea that underlies everything in this section of the book.

Not everyone can do everything.
But everyone can do something.

And when millions of people do something, outcomes change.

Part 2 is designed to help you move from awareness to action without assuming you have a sustainability job title, unlimited influence, or the freedom to start again from scratch. It is written for the student deciding what to study; the apprentice learning on site; the nurse on a night shift; the retail worker on their feet all day; the IT analyst staring at dashboards; the parent juggling school lunches; the accountant building a spreadsheet that will quietly shape a million-dollar decision; and the senior leader with real influence and a calendar that never seems to empty.

By the end of Part 2, you should have a clearer sense of where your skills and interests intersect with climate action, a better understanding of how change actually happens inside organisations and communities, confidence that influence does not require perfection or permission, and at least one practical action you can take from where you are.

That is enough to begin.

A Just Transition

There is a well-known saying in climate circles: "There are no jobs on a dead planet." It is sharp, and it is true.

But it only tells half the story.

Yes, ecological collapse threatens livelihoods worldwide. Yet the transition to a low-carbon economy also creates huge potential for new jobs, new industries, and a fairer economy, if people move with the system rather than being left behind by it. This is what people mean when they talk about a "just transition": cutting emissions quickly, while being honest about who carries the costs, who shares in the benefits, and who needs support along the way.

Mary Robinson has called climate change "the greatest threat to human rights in the 21st century." The point is simple: solving this is not only a technical challenge. It is a justice challenge. The goal is not just to decarbonise quickly; it is to do it in a way that strengthens resilience, protects communities, and shares the benefits of change.

A just transition is not a theory. It is the difference between a future that feels like a shared project and one that feels like theft.

It means telling the truth about what changes. Some industries that once drove prosperity will decline, particularly those dependent on fossil fuels. Propping up yesterday's jobs can delay the inevitable and make the eventual shift more abrupt and painful. The better approach is twofold: build the future and support the people affected.

Building the future means expanding clean energy, electrifying transport and heating, upgrading housing, investing in low-carbon construction, restoring ecosystems, improving public transport, redesigning food systems, making industry more efficient, and building cities that keep people safe in a hotter world.

Supporting the people affected means retraining programmes that lead to real jobs, income support where needed, portable qualifications, apprenticeships, and investment in regions that could otherwise be stranded.

A just transition also means noticing who is already carrying too much.

If you work in healthcare, you may already be seeing how extreme heat, storms, mouldy housing, and energy poverty show up as real patients with real symptoms. If you work in community services, you may be supporting people whose lives are shaped by instability, and climate-driven shocks are just another layer of pressure. If you work in retail, you will feel cost volatility in supply chains and food systems long before it makes the evening news. If you work in IT, you may find yourself balancing rising data demands with energy efficiency and responsible infrastructure choices. If you work in the arts, you may be trying to tell stories that cut through apathy and misinformation, while the world itself becomes harder to tour, fund, and insure. If you work in horticulture or agriculture, you are literally in the weather business now, whether you asked to be or not.

The transition touches everything.

Not everyone can redesign policy or overhaul job markets. But almost everyone can prepare. As a worker, student, tradesperson, designer, manager, nurse, analyst, accountant, developer, or artist, now is a good time to future-proof yourself: upskill, cross-train, stay informed about your sector's direction of travel, and aim your career toward solutions that will still be needed in ten, twenty, or thirty years.

Climate action must be fast. But it must also be fair. Otherwise, we risk tackling the problem and losing the people we need to carry the solution.

And it is hard to build a better world with people who are burnt-out.

Which brings us neatly to the starting line.

How to Begin

Before we get tactical, it helps to be clear about what you are aiming for, and why. This part of the book explores different pathways depending on your career stage, role, and circumstances. But before any of that, we start with you.

Three questions do most of the heavy lifting.

First: Why do you want to do this?
Part 1 likely helped here. You do not need a polished mission statement; you need an honest sense of what is pulling you toward this work. For some people, it is fear, or anger, or grief. For others it is love, curiosity, justice, or a stubborn refusal to accept that "this is just how things are."

Second: What are you trying to achieve?
Are you aiming to influence your current workplace, build skills, or change direction entirely? Clarity at this stage prevents frustration later. Without it, even good intentions can become scattered and exhausting.

Third: What are your strengths?
Often the hardest step. Many people are modest to a fault, or confident in all the wrong areas. If you are not sure, ask someone who knows you well: a friend, colleague, teacher, coach, or partner. Ask them to reflect back on what you are good at, where you have shown resilience, and what you do that naturally inspires others. Your strengths are the "how" that turns intention into impact.

Two people can share the same motivation and still take completely different paths. A film editor and an electrician might both want a safer, fairer future, but their leverage will look different. That is not a problem. It is the point.

And if you are reading this at fifteen, sixteen, or seventeen, you are not supposed to have a perfect ten-year plan. Most adults do not. Life is messy. People change. Industries shift. Entire job categories appear out of nowhere, usually right after you choose your university subject.

So instead of obsessing over a rigid plan, aim for direction and adaptability. Try things. Notice what energises you and what drains you. Build skills that travel well: communication, collaboration, problem-solving, empathy, and the ability to learn quickly. Those are climate skills, too.

You do not have to choose your whole life at seventeen. You just have to choose a next step, no mater how big or small.

Find your climate niche

The Japanese concept of Ikigai (discussed in Part 1) is the overlap of what you enjoy, what you are good at, what the world needs, and what you can be paid for. It gets overused on social media, usually paired with a neat Venn diagram and the implication that if you just "find your Ikigai," you will wake up every day glowing with purpose. Real life is not that tidy.

But as a compass, it is useful.

It also loops neatly back to two ideas we have already touched: find your why (Part 1), and find your niche (this part).

Your "why" is the fuel. Your niche is where you put that energy to work. And ikigai sits in the overlap, the place that makes the work sustainable, not just morally satisfying for a year or two, but liveable over the long haul.

If you care about climate because you want healthier homes, your niche might sit in building design, ventilation, retrofitting, or public health. If what drives you is anger at inequality, you might gravitate toward policy, community services, housing advocacy, or programmes that tackle energy poverty. If you care because you love the natural world, your place might be conservation, ecology, supply chains, or regenerative horticulture. If you are fascinated by systems and incentives, you might find yourself in finance, governance, or the very unglamorous but deeply powerful world of procurement and compliance. And if you are a storyteller at heart, your niche might be film, media, journalism, or art that quietly shifts how people see the world.

Ikigai is not a job title.
It is a direction.

And it is not something you discover once. It is something you revisit. It changes as you change.

At seventeen, your Ikigai might simply be: "I like making things, I like working with people, I like being outdoors, and I want a future that makes sense." Great. That is a strong start. You can build from there.

At forty seven, your Ikigai might be: "I am good at managing teams and budgets, I am tired of wasting my life on meaningless work, and I want to leave things better than I found them." Also great. Also a start.

Here is the reassuring bit: the future needs climate scientists and climate-smart creatives, coders, lawyers, farmers, accountants, nurses, tradies, engineers, marketers, teachers, storytellers, designers, and yes, even procurement managers (because someone has to stop the organisation buying the same rubbish forever).

Climate work is not a single lane. It is a whole motorway system.

Pick an entry road.

The Three Paths in Practice

We have named the three paths. Now, let us make them real.

Because "start where you are" sounds inspiring until you are actually at work on a Tuesday, trying to get through your tasks, and someone asks you to "just quickly" join a meeting that could have been an email.

So, we are going to walk through each path, not as an abstract idea, but as a practical approach you can take in your life, in your job, and in your community.

Along the way, we will revisit a few themes repeatedly, because they are the hidden mechanics of change: curiosity, connection, communication, and persistence.

Path 1: Start Where You Are

This is the most underestimated path, and arguably the most important. It is the path of influence without reinvention.

It looks like noticing what your workplace or community actually does, understanding where the biggest impacts sit, asking better questions, nudging decisions toward better outcomes, and making change feel normal rather than heroic.

That applies whether you work in a corporate office, a café, a hospital ward, a farm, a classroom, a construction site, a theatre, a call centre, or a supermarket.

Starting where you are does not mean small. It means local. It means grounded in what you can actually touch.

This idea is central to Project Drawdown's work, which I mentioned earlier for good reason. Drawdown's research consistently shows that meaningful climate progress comes from aligning everyday decisions with proven solutions, not from grand gestures, but from ordinary roles connected to real systems. Their work helped me realise that climate action does not begin with a job title. It starts with attention.

If you work in hospitality, this may include menu choices, food waste, supplier selection, energy use in kitchens, and event operations. It may mean switching to tap water instead of plastic bottles. It might mean working with local producers and normalising the use of seasonal ingredients. It might also mean protecting staff, because a just transition is not only about carbon. It is about people being treated like human beings.

If you work in education, it might mean weaving climate literacy into existing subjects, supporting students to ask better questions, or normalising time in nature as part of wellbeing. It might mean demonstrating to students that climate is not merely a scientific topic. It is also about economics, design, health, politics, culture, and justice.

If you work in the arts, film, or media, this may mean adopting low-impact production practices, reducing travel and waste on set, reusing materials, or telling climate stories without preaching. Sometimes the most powerful shift is simply telling the truth in a way people can feel.

If you are a student, starting where you are might mean asking what your course is actually teaching you about the future you are entering. It might mean choosing a project that forces you to learn something useful. It might mean joining a club, volunteering, or reaching out to someone doing work you respect and asking how they got there. It might also mean recognising what brings you alive, because career decisions made out of fear tend to lead to burnout.

The key idea is this: every sector has levers.

Your job is to spot them. You do not have to pull all of them. You just have to start pulling one.

This is what starting where you are usually looks like in practice.
Less "save the planet", more "why are we paying for this?"

Starting where you are is not just about motivation or good intentions. It's about building habits that quietly compound over time.

The first habit is learning to see systems. Noticing how decisions are really made, what gets measured, who signs things off, and where the friction actually sits.

The second habit is asking better questions. Not the kind that puts people on the defensive, but the type that opens conversations and invites curiosity.

The third habit is trust. People do not back your ideas simply because they are right. They back them because they trust you. Trust is built slowly, through competence, consistency, and respect.

The fourth habit is framing and learning to articulate the same idea in ways different people can understand. What lands with an engineer will not land with a finance manager.

The fifth habit is small action. Taking steps that are realistic, low risk, and repeatable. Trying something, learning from it, and improving it.

This is exactly the pattern Project Drawdown points to again and again. Do the doable. Repeat what works. Scale it where you can.

Starting where you are is not a motivational poster.
It is a strategy.

And for most people, it is the most accessible place to begin.

Because it does not require you to quit your job, move city, retrain, or become someone else.

It requires you to pay attention.

And paying attention is a superpower.

Path 2: Build Climate and Sustainability into Your Skillset

This path is about capability.

It is about learning enough to participate, then learning enough to lead.

It can be formal, but it does not have to be. It can be a short course, a micro-credential, a certificate, a project, a volunteer role, a series of books, or simply a consistent habit of learning. The aim is to become literate in the language of change.

If you are early in your career, the advantage is flexibility. You can choose projects and subjects aligned with the future, not the past. If you are later in your career, your advantage is context. You already understand how decisions are made, how budgets work, how people behave under pressure, and how organisations resist change. Adding climate literacy makes you a translator who can shift real decisions.

There is also a simple truth: many "green jobs" are not entirely new jobs. They are existing jobs reshaped. The builder who learns airtightness and retrofit becomes part of the solution. The nurse who understands the impacts of climate health becomes essential. The accountant who understands climate risk becomes a quiet climate leader. The teacher who builds climate literacy among students is shaping future voters, consumers, and decision-makers. The software engineer who develops tools to measure energy use is enabling better decisions across entire systems.

Many people get stuck at this stage because they think they need to become an expert before they can act.

You do not.

You need enough knowledge to stop guessing and the courage to ask questions.

One of the most significant barriers to people entering climate work is the belief that there is a "correct" pathway. There is not.

Some people studied environmental science. Some studied engineering. Some studied economics. Some studied law. Some studied art.

Some studied nothing and learned on the job. Some switched careers at thirty. Some switched at fifty. Some never "switched" at all; they just started doing better work in their existing role.

Climate work is not a club with a single entrance door.

It is a messy, evolving field of people learning in public.

If someone tells you that they have it all figured out, gently smile and back away.

If you are building your skill set, it helps to know which skills are consistently valuable across sectors.

Technical knowledge matters. Data matters. Carbon accounting matters. Policy matters. Engineering matters.

But the skills that repeatedly distinguish people who create change from people who merely understand the problem are often "soft skills", which is an insulting phrase, because they are some of the hardest skills to build.

Communication. Negotiation. Collaboration. Stakeholder engagement. Listening. The ability to stay calm in a room full of stressed people.

Climate action is technical, yes. It is also relational.

A person who can explain a complex idea clearly, build trust, and bring people together is often more valuable than someone who can recite a hundred facts.

Not because facts do not matter, but because facts do not implement themselves.

Path 3: Change Roles, Organisations, or Sectors

This is the path of reinvention. It can be powerful. It can also be hard.

Some people pivot because their organisation is moving too slowly, or because their values no longer align with what the organisation does. Some pivot because they want to work directly on solutions. Some pivot because a personal moment changes their priorities.

This path can come with trade-offs: salary changes, uncertainty, becoming a beginner again, and risks not everyone can afford. There is no shame in choosing it, nor in not choosing it.

A gentle warning: climate and sustainability jobs are not automatically healthy jobs. Some are brilliant. Some are chaotic. Some are underfunded and exhausting. Some organisations have excellent marketing and weaker substance. If you pivot, do it with eyes open. Values matter—culture matters. Real impact matters.

And sometimes the best pivot is not into a "climate job" at all, but into a role aligned with the future and that gives you a platform to influence. A role in procurement that shifts supply chains. A role in product design that reduces materials. A role in urban planning that improves transport and housing. A role in media that shifts narratives. A role in finance that changes what gets funded.

Do not get too attached to labels.

Get attached to leverage.

The Hidden Mechanics of Change

Before we get into specific tools and steps, we need to address something that almost no one likes talking about. Influence.

Whether you start where you are, build skills, or pivot, you will run into the same reality: change depends on people.

Even the most brilliant technical solution fails if nobody adopts it, and this is where a lot of climate work unexpectedly resembles sales.

Stay with me...

You Are Already in Sales (Yes, Even You)

Most change depends on influence: how ideas travel, land, and turn into decisions.

When we say 'sales', I know what you're picturing: a used-car salesperson by the name of Harry Wormwood explaining why you do not actually need all four wheels. Or someone enthusiastically promoting double glazing while standing outside your house, which already has double-glazed windows.

But stay with me.

The word "sales" carries baggage. And yet, some of the most principled, thoughtful, genuinely helpful people I have worked with have been in sales. The best salespeople do not push what is wrong for the customer. They help people make better decisions. They earn trust, and repeat business follows.

Here is the punchline: you have already been doing sales, whether or not it appears on your business card.

If you have ever interviewed for a job, asked for a promotion, pitched an idea, tried to change a process, advocated for a patient, persuaded a director, encouraged a teammate, convinced your parents to let you switch subjects, or tried to get your friend to vote, you have been selling something. A decision. A direction. A change.

Climate work is full of this. Communication and translation.

Some people tune out when they hear "climate change". Others tune out when they hear "sustainability". Some people respond to cost. Some respond to health. Some react to pride and legacy. Some respond to fairness. Some respond to being shown what competitors are doing.

If you want to influence change, you learn to speak multiple languages. Not different spoken languages, though those help too. Different human languages: data, story, risk, reputation, cost, wellbeing, security, purpose.

You do not have to become a salesperson. You have to become a translator.

And yes, that includes the awkward conversation at Christmas.

You cannot spreadsheet your uncle into accepting reality.

But you might be able to move the conversation from "global conspiracy" to "lower bills and healthier homes", which is sometimes as close as you get to progress.

Connection Matters More Than Charisma

We operate in a system that rewards confident presenters and loud voices. But impact does not require you to become the loudest person in the room. Quiet influence is still influence.

What matters is connection. People follow people they trust.

If pitching ideas feels daunting, find one ally first. Practice one sentence that explains what you care about and why it matters. Adjust your approach to the person in front of you. Some respond to data. Some respond to stories. Some react to practicality. Some respond to identity and values.

Adapting your approach does not mean compromising who you are. It means strengthening how you connect.

And while we are here, a reminder: role models and mentors are not only found in workplaces.

Sometimes the person who changes your life is a teacher. Sometimes your role model is family.

An English teacher who inspires you to write a (climate) book. Or a sister who teaches you more about leadership than any podcast ever could.

Mentors can be a coach, a colleague, a community elder, a manager who backs you early, or a friend who tells you the truth gently when you need it.

Your people are part of your climate toolkit.

Which brings us to a practical question.

What do you actually do next?

A Practical Path

The steps below are tools, not commandments. Use what fits your world, adapt what does not, and do not worry about doing them in the "correct" order.

The point is not about perfection, it's about progress.

1. Learn the ground you are standing on

If you want to shift your workplace or community, start with the basics:

What are we actually doing right now?

Have we made commitments? Do we measure anything meaningful? Do we report on emissions or energy use? Does "environmental strategy" exist outside a brochure? Are we ahead of the competition, or behaving as if it's 1999?

If you do not work in an office, the same applies. Whether you are in healthcare, trades, hospitality, social care, education, retail, or creative work, sustainability shows up in the products you use, the waste you generate, the suppliers you choose, the energy you burn, the travel you do, and the decisions leaders make without thinking twice.

Then zoom out.

Look at your sector. Look at your country. Look globally if you can; even just headlines help.

What regulations are coming? What technologies are shifting expectations? What are customers or communities asking for? What is becoming normal elsewhere that has not yet reached your workplace?

You do not need deep expertise. You need enough awareness to stop guessing.

Understanding the system you are in shows you where the levers are.

And where they are not.

2. Build yourself an education (without needing a PhD)

Nobody arrives in climate work fully qualified. If they claim they did, they are either lying or were raised by IPCC scientists.

Start small.

Free courses, podcasts, newsletters, webinars, accessible introductions to climate science, climate literacy, or sector-specific topics.

Go bigger only if you want to.

Postgraduate programmes, micro-credentials, or leadership courses are brilliant for some people and completely unrealistic for others. Both are valid.

Education is not about knowing everything. It is about knowing enough to participate.

If you are early in your career, learning the basics helps you build credibility.

If you are later in your career, especially in leadership, it is essential because climate and nature disclosure frameworks are becoming mandatory, and misunderstanding them carries real business, financial, and governance risk.

3. Find your people

You need people: role models, peers, allies, encouragers, challengers, the ones who remind you to breathe when things move too slowly, and the ones who remind you to rest when you are about to sprint into burnout.

Role models matter. Not because you mimic their path, but because they show you what is possible.

Mentors matter too, and they do not need to last forever. Different stages of your career require different types of support. Some mentors give confidence, some give honesty, some give the exact sentence you need right before a difficult meeting.

Advocates matter as well. Advocates are the individuals in senior rooms who say, "We need your name in this meeting." They use their influence to open doors you cannot yet reach. Advocacy is not charity; it is correcting imbalance and noticing whose voices are missing.

If you are in a position of influence, use it. Invite people in. Make space. Say the name of the person who is not in the room but should be.

If you do not yet have that network, build it gradually. Reach out to one person. Attend one event. Join one working group. Even one connection is a seed that grows.

4. Understand the landscape you are operating in

Whatever sector you are in, someone somewhere is already doing something better than your organisation. That can be frustrating, or incredibly useful.

If you work in hospitality, which venues are reducing waste and working with local suppliers?

If you work in construction, which firms have shifted to electric tools or low-carbon material selection?
If you work in retail, which stores donate surplus food rather than discard it?
If you work in media, who is telling climate stories without losing audiences?

Evidence matters, especially for decision-makers who tune out moral arguments but tune in to risk, trends, reputation, and market pressure.

Seeing what is possible elsewhere gives you leverage at home.

5. Start small before your brain convinces you that you are unqualified

Most climate action inside a workplace begins with a question that feels almost too simple:

"Do we have a plan for this?"
"Could we donate this instead of binning it?"
"Has anyone looked into electrifying the fleet?"
"What would it take to pilot this idea?"

Small actions create credibility. Credibility creates trust. Trust creates bigger actions.

Imposter syndrome will tell you that you are not ready, not knowledgeable, not senior enough, not the "right person" to raise the idea.

Do it anyway.

No one undertaking meaningful sustainability work feels fully ready. They feel responsible, which is much more helpful.

6. *Know who has power, and who has heart*

Meaningful change rarely starts with a committee.

It starts with a few people who care.

Notice who those people are.

Some will have influence, budget, authority, and positional power. Some will have allyship, enthusiasm, passion, and curiosity. Occasionally, you will find someone who has both, and that person becomes your internal secret weapon.

Quiet influence is still influence. People listen to those who make them feel safe, not pressured.

7. *Make it strategic, not personal*

As your work grows, sustainability needs to shift from "a good idea" to "a business priority".

That means connecting your ideas to what leaders care about: risk, cost, compliance, reputation, talent, customer expectations, competitive advantage, safety, and reliability.

You are not watering down the moral argument. You are widening the audience for it.

Remember that power exists everywhere within an organisation.

A supply chain manager changing procurement criteria can shift emissions more than a CEO's speech.
A teacher shapes a generation.
A supermarket worker advocating for food donation changes waste systems.
An entry-level employee can change conversations.
A senior leader can change culture and priorities.

Your job is to spot where your influence sits and use it.

The 30-Day Starter Plan

Climate action at work does not begin with a grand strategy. It begins with movement.

Action gets easier when you break big, overwhelming problems into *small, time-bounded questions*. That's the insight behind the "by Friday" mindset — the idea that short horizons make complex change feel less like a mountain and more like a next step you can actually take. You don't need to have all the answers yet. You just need a next action you can complete *by Friday*.

This simple 30-day framework isn't a productivity challenge or a test of commitment. It's a way to turn curiosity into confidence, one small step at a time.

Many people stall because "solve climate change" is too big to hold in your head. A simple weekly horizon turns anxiety into something you can actually do. Rather than trying to fix everything at once, you focus on the next practical step you can take in the short term. When you stack these actions week by week, you build momentum without the stress of getting it *perfect*.

You can adapt this plan to your role, your energy levels, and your constraints. The only rule is to keep it realistic.

If you want a deeper, more comprehensive companion to this starter plan, organisations like Climate Voice offer excellent employee climate action guides that expand on many of these ideas. This plan is designed to help you start; their resources help you go further.

Week 1: Learn the ground you are standing on
Pay attention. Notice how decisions are made in your workplace or sector.
Read one or two credible sources related to your industry and climate.
Look at what your organisation already says it is doing, and what it doesn't mention at all.

Week 1 output: One short paragraph: *This is how my workplace currently works.*

You're not trying to fix anything yet. You're learning the system.

Week 2: Find one person and one example
Identify one person who might care, or who is at least open to the conversation.
This could be a colleague, manager, peer, teacher, or external contact.

At the same time, find one example of a company, team, or organisation doing something better than yours. Not perfect. Just better.

Week 2 output: One ally, and one external example.

Week 3: Take one small action
Choose one low-risk, practical step.
Ask a question. Share an article. Suggest a pilot. Start a conversation.
Reframe an idea in language that resonates with decision-makers.

Week 3 output: One small action taken.

Week 4: Reflect and decide what comes next
What worked?
What felt uncomfortable?
Who responded positively?
What surprised you?

Week 4 output: One decision: *repeat, scale, shift, or pause.*

You're not assessing success or failure. You're gathering information.

Progress is rarely linear. Momentum comes from learning, adjusting, and continuing.

You don't need to do everything.
You don't need to move fast all the time.
You only need to start.

Keep going

In the section we have just covered, we talked about learning the ground you are standing on, finding allies, building your understanding, and starting small. None of that works in isolation. It works because of people.

Finding allies matters. Change is heavy when you try to carry it alone. One colleague who nods when you speak. One manager who is willing to listen. One person who says, "I've been thinking the same thing." That is how momentum begins. Quietly. Gradually. Collectively.

We also spoke about discovering your "why". That part is not optional. Tactics without purpose fade quickly. When things get awkward, slow, political, or frustrating, and they will, your "why" is what steadies you. It is what reminds you why you are having the conversation in the first place.

If you are reading this book, I am going to assume you already care. You probably already feel that restless nudge that says, "We could do better than this." Use that.

Many people are going through the motions at work. Turning up, doing the job, collecting the pay cheque, and counting down to Friday. And the pay cheque matters. Stability matters. Life is expensive. But meaning matters too.

We need people who are willing to bring energy into rooms that feel flat. People who are curious enough to ask questions. People who are optimistic enough to imagine something better, and stubborn enough to keep nudging toward it.

You do not have to be the loudest voice. You do not have to change everything at once. Sometimes progress is two steps forward and one step back. That's life. Use the frameworks and examples in this section if they help.

This work is not reserved for sustainability managers or policy experts. It needs engineers and nurses, teachers and tradies, marketers and mechanics, bankers and baristas. It needs introverts and extroverts. It needs steady thinkers and bold experimenters.

Bring your passion. Bring your skills. Bring your perspective.

We are not looking for perfection. We are building momentum.

And momentum is a powerful thing.

A few years ago, I read Chapter One by Daniel Flynn, and the story stayed with me.

If you live in Australia or New Zealand, you'll probably know the Thankyou brand. You've likely seen their cosmetics or household products on supermarket shelves. And if you rewind far enough, you might remember their original product: bottled water.

A few young people looked at a global problem, extreme poverty and lack of access to clean water, and decided to do something about it. They created a product and directed the profits toward funding clean water projects.

They were not seasoned business professionals. They did not have decades of supply chain experience or deep capital reserves. What they had was clarity of purpose and the willingness to begin.

And that is the part that matters: They cared. They got started.

They faced rejection from major retailers. They navigated funding challenges, logistics hurdles, and constant uncertainty. But the company grew. It became a recognisable brand. It funded real, tangible outcomes for communities.

And then something interesting happened.

As awareness of plastic waste and its environmental impact grew, they began to question their own model. Yes, the profits were doing good. But they were still producing single-use bottled water. Eventually, they decided to pivot away from it.

That decision wouldn't have been easy. It takes transparency. It takes the ability to say, "This made sense at the time. It might not make sense now."

That is climate work.

Do your research. Understand the system. Find your why. Then get started.

You will make mistakes. You will underestimate things. You will probably overestimate other things. That is not a sign that you should not have tried.

The real test is not whether you get it perfect first time. It is whether you are willing to notice when something can be better and making the effort to change and adapt.

Progress is rarely clean. But it is built by people who care enough to begin.

When Organisations Lead Before Policy

Some of the most meaningful climate progress does not begin with regulation. It starts when organisations choose to move early and bring others with them, often across sectors and competitive boundaries.

Industry-wide initiatives such as the Clean Cooling Collaborative in the United States, the Mercury Consortium in the United Kingdom and Europe, and Aotearoa New Zealand's Energy Transition Framework show what this can look like in practice. These efforts are not fringe experiments. They bring together companies, technical partners, and system actors to tackle barriers before policy forces their hand.

The Clean Cooling Collaborative works to transform the global cooling sector (one of the fastest-growing sources of energy demand) by scaling efficient, climate-friendly cooling solutions and aligning finance, policy, and technology. It collaborates with partners such as ACEEE, Carbon Trust, Cool Coalition, RMI, and NRDC, as well as industry bodies and standards organisations to drive gigaton-scale emissions reductions and equitable access to cooling technology.

The Mercury Consortium is a nonprofit collaborative focused on accelerating interoperability across distributed energy resources (DER), such as EV chargers, heat pumps, batteries, and smart thermostats, so these technologies work together rather than in silos. It brings together Kraken, Octopus, EDF, UK Power Networks, Daikin, and other manufacturers, utilities, regulators, and tech providers to develop shared specifications and technical guidelines, unlocking greater consumer participation and system flexibility.

In Aotearoa New Zealand, the Energy Transition Framework unites more than 30 energy-sector participants, from generators and retailers to lines companies, distributors, and independent advisors, to coordinate collective action on decarbonisation, resilience, electricity security, and affordability. Members include major firms such as Transpower, Mercury, Genesis, and Contact, as well as independent organisations representing consumers, and infrastructure groups connected to the national grid.

What connects these examples is not just ambition, but how they came into being. They rarely start with a single heroic organisation or a perfectly timed policy signal. More often, they begin with people within organisations who identify a gap, have an idea, and are willing to undertake the hard, unglamorous work of bringing others together.

This is leadership as it most often shows up in the real world: not through titles or speeches, but through collaboration, persistence, and a willingness to work well with others.

Values must align. Communication must be clear. Trust must be built across competing interests. The organisations matter, but so do the individuals willing to pick up the phone, organise the meeting, write the first draft, absorb the criticism, and keep going.

And this is worth saying plainly: if you are waiting for perfect policy before acting, you may be waiting a long time.

Sometimes policy follows leadership. Sometimes policy follows culture. Sometimes policy follows competition. Sometimes, policy follows a crisis. It is better to lead before the crisis makes it non-negotiable.

A Different Path to Impact (NGOs)

Many people think that if they want to help solve the climate crisis, their only option is to work in the "sustainability divisions" of large firms, or to specialise in engineering, energy, or green tech. There's another (often-overlooked) route: working for an NGO or grassroots organisation.

NGOs aren't just "do-gooder hobby clubs." As Patagonia's *Tools for Grassroots Activists* emphasises, they operate in the same ecosystem as businesses. They must master many of the same tools: strategy, marketing, community-building, communications, fundraising, and advocacy.

NGOs "sell" a different kind of product — the vision of clean water, healthy ecosystems, fair communities — but selling a vision requires rigour, discipline and transparent organisational structure, just like any business.

Systemic change requires more than installing a more efficient heat pump or switching to renewables. It involves community organising, public pressure, corporate accountability, policy change, and social mobilisation. That's where NGOs have a unique role.

We've already discussed how to identify the right company or role for you in the private sector, but the same principles apply when exploring work in the NGO sector. Whether you're assessing a multinational business or a grassroots organisation, the questions remain similar: Does this align with my values? Is the impact real? And is this an area where I can contribute meaningfully to the change I want to see?

When looking for opportunities, it might be worth reaching out to a recruiter in the space, or searching for job boards that specifically focus on NGO, or Impact work, such as Do Good Jobs (Work with Purpose | Mahi ki te Kaupapa) in Aotearoa New Zealand. If you're getting stuck, try a different approach. Perhaps you could research an industry or organisation you're interested in and see if any of their staff are active on platforms like LinkedIn, reach out, be yourself but also be patient, sometimes building connections or job opportunities can take a long time to develop.

Employers Opportunity

If you've made it this far and you're an employer, you might be wondering: What is my role in all of this?

The short answer is that it's huge.

You provide employment. In uncertain economic and climatic times, that alone matters. You shape daily routines, financial security, wellbeing, mobility patterns, consumption habits, and workplace culture for dozens, hundreds, or sometimes thousands of people. Few roles carry that much quiet influence.

You may not be ready to transform your company into a climate-positive, regenerative organisation overnight. That is fine. Leadership does not begin with perfection. It begins with intent and action.

Start with what you directly control.

Research on workplace ESG consistently shows that employees experience sustainability not just through environmental policies, but through how fairly, safely, and flexibly they are treated. Social impact and environmental impact overlap more than many employers realise.

Some practical places to begin:

Create inclusive and supportive work policies.
Gender-neutral parental leave, caregiver leave, and flexible return-to-work arrangements reduce inequality and improve long-term workforce participation, especially for women, who still carry a disproportionate share of unpaid care work. These policies are not just socially responsible. They strengthen retention, loyalty, and productivity.

Normalise flexible and remote work where possible.
Flexible hours and remote or hybrid options reduce commuting emissions, ease pressure on families, and improve wellbeing. They also expand access to employment for people with disabilities, caregivers, and those outside major cities.

Invest in wellbeing and psychological safety.
Burnout, stress, and disengagement are not separate from climate. Teams that feel safe, supported, and heard are more

willing to innovate, speak up, and adapt. Simple policies around mental health support, reasonable workloads, and clear expectations make a measurable difference.

Pay attention to procurement and everyday operations. Even small changes matter. Choosing lower-impact suppliers, reducing waste, improving energy efficiency in offices and warehouses, and switching to renewable electricity where available are visible signals that values translate into action.

Give people permission to care.
Encourage staff to contribute ideas. Support internal climate or sustainability working groups. Allow time for volunteering or community engagement. Culture changes faster when people feel ownership rather than instruction.

Best practice organisations often go further: embedding ESG into performance frameworks, linking leadership incentives to sustainability outcomes, and transparently reporting progress. But you do not need to start there.

The most important step is recognising that your business is not separate from society. It is part of it.

You don't need to wait for regulation to tell you how to care for your workforce. You don't need perfect data before improving workplace culture. And you don't need a sustainability department to lead with values.

Just as with engineers, financiers, and teachers, climate leadership inside organisations usually begins with small, human decisions: how people are treated, what is prioritised, and what behaviours are rewarded.

Employers shape more than balance sheets. They shape lives. And that makes your job a climate job too.

And there is another practical reality worth acknowledging. As climate awareness grows, so does competition for skilled workers who want their work to align with their values. Organisations that invest in inclusive policies, flexible work, wellbeing, and genuine sustainability action increasingly position themselves as employers of choice. For many people, especially younger generations and highly skilled professionals, workplace culture and purpose now sit alongside salary and job title when choosing where to work.

This does not make these changes cynical or transactional. For many employers, treating people well is simply basic decency. But if the outcome is a healthier workplace, stronger retention, higher engagement, and a more motivated workforce, then that is not a contradiction. It is alignment.

Doing the right thing and building a better business do not have to be opposing goals. Sometimes, they are the same thing.

For Teachers

"If children don't grow up learning about and appreciating nature, they won't understand its importance, they won't protect it — and then who will?" — David Attenborough.

A powerful reminder of the influence teachers, parents, caregivers and youth workers hold.

Whether you teach five-year-olds, university students, or apprentices learning a trade, you have an extraordinary opportunity and, dare I say, a responsibility to help shape how the next generation understands the world they're inheriting. Climate change can feel overwhelming, but your role is not to provide all the answers. It is to spark curiosity. To nurture empathy. To help young people see that the natural world is not separate from human life, but deeply intertwined with it.

One of the most overlooked truths about climate action is that social impact is often environmental impact. Research highlighted by Project Drawdown shows that education, especially for girls and young people from disadvantaged backgrounds, is one of the most powerful long-term levers for climate. Educated communities tend to have better health outcomes, lower vulnerability to climate shocks, stronger economic stability, and greater capacity to adapt. When you support learners who face systemic barriers, you are not just improving individual life outcomes. You are strengthening society's ability to respond to environmental change.

This is what we mean when we say climate work is intersectional. Supporting vulnerable communities, improving access to education, building confidence, and expanding opportunity are all part of building a fairer, more resilient future. Teaching is climate action, even when the lesson is not explicitly about carbon.

And this does not require rewriting your entire curriculum. It can be as simple as asking better questions: Where does this material come from? Why does design matter? What happens to something when we throw it away? How is this species, this ecosystem, this technology connected to everything else? Every subject — science, art, economics, engineering, literature, hospitality, geography, construction — has threads that link back to people and planet.

Equally important is how you teach, not just what you teach. Be the teacher who inspires. Who makes students feel safe to ask questions, to fail, to experiment, to try again. Encourage curiosity. Support confidence. Create classrooms and workshops where young people feel seen, valued, and capable of shaping their own futures.

And wherever possible, offer opportunities to connect with the natural world itself. A walk outside. A school garden. A restored stream. A local park. These moments matter. People protect what they know. They protect what they love.

Teachers do not just shape careers. They shape worldviews. And if we want a future full of people who understand the value of ecosystems, communities, and the climate we all share, that understanding begins long before anyone enters the workforce. It begins in classrooms, workshops, playgrounds, and homes, one conversation at a time.

For Students

If you are reading this while studying, whether you are at a university about to start an architecture degree, at a Trades college learning motor vehicle maintenance, or in high school trying to work out what on earth you are meant to do with your life, here is something worth doing early:

Look closely at what your course is actually teaching you about the future you will be working in.

Open the course handbook. Read the module outlines. Ask questions.

How does your programme teach climate and sustainability? How does it talk about risk, adaptation and resilience? What skills is it preparing you for, and are they the skills the world will still need in ten years?

If you are halfway through your course and climate has not been mentioned once, that is not a sign to panic. It is, however, a brilliant moment to ask a lecturer or tutor how this can be woven into your learning.

Educators do not have all the answers. Many are trying to update decades-old curricula while coping with limited resources and rapidly changing industries. Sometimes it only takes one student asking the right question for a whole class to benefit.

Because whatever career path you are preparing for, climate change will shape it.

Architects should be trained in low-carbon design, material impacts, retrofitting, and the design of buildings that withstand heatwaves and storms.
Mechanics should be learning about EVs and electrification.
Business students should learn about climate risk and disclosure.
Nursing and medical students should understand climate-related health conditions.
IT students should understand the energy demand of digital infrastructure and the ethics of AI.
Agriculture and horticulture students should learn about drought resilience and soil health.
Engineering students should explore electrification, low-carbon materials, and systems thinking.
Legal students should be exposed to climate litigation and regulation.
Marketing students should be taught about greenwashing and truthful communication.
Film and media students should be learning how to tell complex stories without losing the audience.

The point is simple: every field is changing.

Your education is the foundation. Your curiosity is the accelerant. And your voice, even now, can shape how your profession evolves.

And if you still feel lost, remember this: at seventeen years old, no one has a perfect plan. The goal is not certainty. The goal is direction. Try things. Keep what fits. Let yourself change.

Because learning does not stop when formal education ends, for many people, the next phase of influence happens not in lecture theatres or workplaces, but much closer to home.

Stay-at-Home Parents

Let's be clear from the start: climate impact isn't reserved for people in boardrooms, labs, or policy forums. Sometimes it happens at the kitchen table, between packing lunches and negotiating bedtime.

While the data show that mothers are still far more likely to be stay-at-home parents than fathers, this section is for anyone doing the work of keeping a household running, regardless of gender.

At the time of writing, around 20% of mothers in Australia are stay-at-home parents, compared to about 3.8% of fathers. That gap reflects long-standing expectations and uneven pressures. Women still carry a disproportionate share of unpaid care and domestic work, and that imbalance is not just a gender issue. It is an inequality issue.

And inequality and climate are closely linked. When people are stretched, underpaid, or unsupported, their ability to make long-term choices declines. You cannot ask families to "live sustainably" in a system that makes everyday life a sprint.

But here is the flip side: running a household is a position of real leverage.

Stay-at-home parents often manage the household budget, food choices, energy use, clothing purchases, transport logistics, and the day-to-day decisions that shape demand. You do not need a sustainability title to make a difference if you are the person deciding what gets bought, what gets binned, and what becomes "normal" in your home.

Small shifts add up. More plant-forward meals. Second-hand before new. Fewer impulse buys—less food waste. Repair over replace. Supporting local businesses when you can. Every purchase is, quite literally, a tiny vote for the world your children will inherit.

And speaking of children, influence does not get much bigger than shaping the habits of the next generation. Children absorb routines quickly, especially those they observe repeatedly. Teaching them to turn off lights, ask where things come from, separate waste, care for nature, and recognise marketing tactics is long-term stewardship. It is not about perfection. It is about raising people who instinctively ask, "Does this make sense?"

Parenting influence also extends beyond the household. Stay-at-home parents often sit at the centre of community networks: schools, sports clubs, playgroups, neighbourhood chats, local Facebook groups, birthday parties, and the informal social infrastructure that holds communities together.

These networks are powerful for normalising change. That might look like pushing for better recycling or lunch-waste systems at school, asking your club to switch suppliers, organising a local clean-up, sharing a helpful resource, or simply being the person who makes climate conversations feel less heavy and more practical. "Here's what worked for us."

One more grounding truth: sustainable family life depends on a society that supports parents. Fair parental leave, flexible work, accessible childcare, safe housing, and decent wages are climate issues too, because they shape what people can realistically do. If one parent is stretched beyond capacity, their ability to plan, engage, and influence shrinks.

Equity is not a side note here. It is foundational.

So whether you are raising children full-time, juggling part-time work, managing the household alongside another job, or caring for whānau in a way that does not fit neatly into a job description, you hold genuine climate influence.

Your decisions today do not just reduce emissions. They shape future voters, consumers, innovators, and leaders.

Because sometimes the most essential climate conversations are not at COP summits.
They are across the dinner table.

And sometimes, despite best efforts at home or at work, people face a more challenging question: where their energy is best spent.

Change Jobs or Change the System?

When it comes to climate action in your career, broadly, there are two approaches: you can start again, or you can start where you are.

Both are valid. Both can have an impact. The real question is:

Do you want to change your job, or change what your job does?

At some point, many people find themselves asking:

"Do I need a complete career shift to make an impact, or can I make a difference right where I am?"

The short answer is: it depends.

The longer answer is: it depends, but you likely have more influence than you realise.

Some people choose to pivot fully. They retrain, study, or transition into industries focused on solutions. This can be deeply rewarding. It can also bring challenges: shifting salary expectations, re-entering beginner mode, or navigating unfamiliar territory.

Others choose to remain in their current roles or industries, not because they lack conviction, but because they recognise the unique leverage they already have. If you work in a sector that must change, you may be well-positioned to help it do so. You may need new skills, but your existing networks, insider knowledge, and organisational trust become powerful tools for change.

Some people go all in on a new career because their company is not moving fast enough, or because the idea of spending the next decade trying to win over leadership feels like running a marathon in gumboots.

Others stay put because they know that if no one in the room pushes for change, nothing will change.

If you thrive on focus and want to dedicate yourself to climate work full-time, a fresh start may be the most energising move you ever make.

If you understand your organisation inside and out and can spot opportunities an outsider might miss, changing the system from within may have a more far-reaching impact.

Ultimately, the decision depends on what you value, what you are willing and able to risk, and where you believe your skills can be most effective.

There is no right choice. There is only your choice.

And you can change it later.

Recruiters: A Tool, not a Shortcut

If you're thinking about changing roles, testing a new direction, or even just trying to understand what options exist, it's worth talking about recruiters.

They get a bad reputation. Sometimes that reputation is entirely deserved.

Plenty of people have stories about being ghosted, misunderstood, or pushed toward roles that clearly were not a good fit. Recruiters work within a system that rewards speed, placement, and volume, not always nuance. So yes, scepticism is healthy.

But every now and then, you find a good one. And when you do, they can be worth their weight in gold.

There is no such thing as a perfect recruiter, just as there is no perfect job. Different people warm to different approaches. Some need reassurance, others need challenge, some want a gentle nudge, others a firm push. As explored later in Part 3 through conversations with people who work inside recruitment, the real value comes from finding someone who listens well enough to meet you where you are, rather than trying to funnel you into a one-size-fits-all path.

I was fortunate early in my career to have a recruiter who reached out at exactly the right moment. They helped me land my first role, but more importantly, they stayed in touch. They checked in. They offered perspective when I felt uncertain. They reminded me to slow down when I was spiralling, and to back myself when I was underestimating my value.

That kind of support is not universal. But it exists.

A good recruiter is not just a job broker. They can help you understand the market, sense-check your CV, translate your experience into language employers recognise, and spot opportunities you might never have found on your own. They often know which companies talk a good game and which ones are actually decent places to work. That insight matters.

They're not for everyone. Some people prefer to navigate job changes independently, and that is completely valid. But if you feel a bit lost, unsure where to look, or overwhelmed by the sheer noise of job boards, a recruiter can be a useful guide.

It helps to think of recruiters a bit like doctors or therapists. You do not assume the first one you meet will be the right fit. Chemistry matters. Trust matters. Values matter. If the first conversation feels off, transactional, or rushed, you are allowed to pivot and try again. That is not failure. It is discernment.

If you do work with a recruiter, be clear about what you want and what you do not want. Tell them what energises you, what drains you, what kind of culture you are trying to avoid, and what kind of work you want to grow into. A good recruiter will listen. A bad one will not.

Used well, recruiters are not a shortcut. They are a tool. One more way to gather information, build networks, and move intentionally rather than blindly.

And if you never find "your" recruiter, that is fine too. This path is not mandatory.

But if you do, and they help you see your own potential more clearly, it can be one of the quieter, steadier forms of support in an otherwise uncertain phase of your career.

Conscious Quitting

Former Unilever CEO Paul Polman has highlighted research showing that many employees want their company to take meaningful climate action, yet believe their leadership does not care.

When organisations do not shift, more people are making that clear in a straightforward way: they leave.

This is not "quiet quitting". It is something more intentional.

Call it values-based quitting. Call it conscious quitting. Call it refusing to spend your life building something you do not believe in.

Leaving is not always possible. Many people cannot afford to quit. Many people have caring responsibilities, financial constraints, immigration constraints, health constraints, or limited job markets. That reality matters, and it deserves respect.

But if you do have a choice, and your workplace is fundamentally misaligned with your values, leaving can be a form of influence too.

It sends a signal.
It protects your energy.

Sometimes influence looks like persuasion.
Sometimes it looks like walking away.

Boundaries and Burnout

Climate work carries a unique emotional load. It deals with long horizons, high stakes, imperfect information, and systems that move more slowly than the science demands. Meaningful work does not protect you from exhaustion.

One of the most common traps people fall into is feeling personally responsible for fixing everything. This is especially true for those who care deeply, notice gaps early, or become the informal "sustainability person" simply by asking a few questions.

A reminder worth repeating:

You are not the system. You are a participant within it.

Sustainable impact requires sustainable effort. That means boundaries. It means saying no. It means avoiding the "unpaid sustainability department" trap. It means choosing longevity over heroics.

Here are a few practical principles.

You are allowed to say no. No to unpaid emotional labour. No to being added to every committee "because you care". No to carrying work that properly belongs to leadership or the organisation itself.

You do not need to move at crisis speed all the time. Climate action does require urgency, but human beings are not built for constant emergency mode. Progress happens in waves: periods of learning, action, frustration, rest, and renewal. That is normal, not a personal weakness.

Protect your role first. Your credibility, energy, and influence come from doing your core job well. If climate work begins to undermine your performance in your primary role, it becomes harder to sustain and easier for others to dismiss. Integrating change into your work is often more powerful than carrying it on top of everything else.

Choose longevity over heroics. The transition will take decades. The people who matter most are not those who burn brightest for a year, but those who stay engaged, adaptable, and healthy over time.

If this work ever feels overwhelming, that does not mean you are unsuited to it. It usually indicates you care and may need support, community, or rest.

A simple boundary check:

Is this mine to carry, or leadership's?
Is this within my role, or is it formally recognised?
Do I have the time and support to do it well?

If the answer is "no" to two or more, it is a signal to pause, renegotiate, or decline.

You might find it useful to borrow a mantra from authors David Benattar and Tony Balfour, who in *What Can We Do by Friday?* encourage us to focus not on being heroes, but on identifying small, doable actions we can take now, repeat, learn from, and improve over time — a practical philosophy that helps us organise and prioritise climate action in daily life and work.

Their book strips away the idea that climate engagement has to be perfect or overwhelming, and instead treats climate action like a series of intentional, incremental moves that anyone (from students and parents to CEOs) can start by Friday.

What "Good" Looks Like in Practice

One of the easiest ways to burn out in climate work is to expect visible, transformative results too quickly.

Real change inside organisations rarely arrives with a press release or a standing ovation. More often, it starts quietly and builds in layers.

Before you measure yourself against unrealistic expectations, it helps to know what progress typically looks like in practice.

After the first month, "good" might look like this: you understand your organisation or sector a little better than you did before, you have found one person who is open to the conversation, and you have identified one idea worth exploring, even if it still feels rough.

After three months, "good" might look like this: you have tested one small action or pilot, a second or third person has shown interest, and you have started to understand what language resonates with decision makers.

After six months, "good" might look like this: you have a clearer business case or pathway for change, a small working group has started to form, and your role in this work is becoming more recognised, even if it is still unofficial.

After a year, "good" might look like this: one idea has moved from conversation to implementation, sustainability considerations are appearing earlier in decisions, and you have a clearer sense of whether you want to deepen this work, formalise it, or shift direction.

If your timeline is slower, that does not mean you are failing. Some systems are bigger. Some risks are higher. Some lives are fuller.

That is not failure. That is context.

The goal is not to race.

It is to stay in the work long enough to matter.

Wrapping Up Part 2: The Work

If Part 1 was about understanding the climate crisis, Part 2 was about working out where *you* sit within it.

By now, I hope you've got a clearer sense of what motivates you, where your skills actually land, and how much influence you already have — even if it doesn't always feel that way. You've hopefully seen that climate action isn't reserved for people with "Head of Sustainability" in their email signature, or for those who know the difference between Scope 2 and Scope 3 without Googling it.

This work happens in real jobs. On messy teams. Inside organisations that are trying to do better. It shows up in meetings, spreadsheets, site visits, policies, procurement decisions, awkward conversations, and the quiet moment when you decide to ask, *"Why do we do it this way?"*

You don't need permission to start.
You don't need a five-year plan, a rebrand, or a perfectly optimised LinkedIn bio.
You mostly need to care about something enough to nudge it in a better direction, repeatedly.

Most change doesn't arrive with a dramatic before-and-after montage. It's incremental. It's imperfect. It often looks like progress only in hindsight. A small tweak. A better default. A question that lingers longer than expected.

And here's the good news: you don't have to abandon what you do.
In many cases, the most impactful thing you can do is *shape* it.

Take the work you already do well and aim it slightly differently. Influence grows through practice, not job titles. And confidence usually arrives *after* you've started, not before.

Climate work isn't just a profession you step into.
It's a practice you build.
A way of showing up.
A habit of paying attention, adjusting course, and sticking with it, even when the progress feels slow or the wins feel underwhelming.

In that sense, it's personal.
And, inconveniently, ongoing.

Part 3: The People

Their Job is a Climate Job

You've now got the context (Part 1) and the toolkit (Part 2).
But no one ever changed the world with a framework alone.

People do that.

The people you're about to meet didn't follow a neat, linear pathway into "climate work". Very few studied environmental science. Even fewer woke up at 18 and confidently announced, *"I shall now embark upon a career in sustainability."*

Their journeys are squiggly. Occasionally accidental, or unplanned.

And far more relatable because of it.

Across these conversations, a common pattern emerges. Each of them noticed something that didn't sit right. A system that could work better. A decision that felt misaligned. A gap between values and reality. And instead of waiting for someone else to fix it, they leaned in, usually starting with the work already in front of them.

That's the point I keep coming back to in this book: every job is a climate job.

Which means that, whether you like it or not, your job is a climate job, too.

These people aren't superheroes[30]. They're busy. They're balancing demanding work, side projects, leadership roles,

---

[30] Though I can't say I've ever seen either of them in the same room as Batman, or Spiderman, so...

families, health, friendships, and the occasional optimistic attempt at rest. Many of these conversations happened across time zones, squeezed between meetings, over rushed lunches, late-night messages, Teams calls, voice notes, and more patience than I probably deserved.

I'm genuinely grateful to every one of them for giving their time so generously.

This section isn't meant to be a set of templates or tidy "career paths to copy". It's not a checklist. And it's definitely not suggesting there's one right way to do this work.

That said, if I'm being honest, it *is* a bit of a hall of fame.

Every person featured here is someone I've crossed paths with along the way. Some I've worked alongside. Some I've met through projects, panels, or conferences. Others appeared via mutual connections, late-night LinkedIn rabbit holes, or a message that started with, *"Hi, sorry to be that person..."*

In different ways, all of them stood out.

They've challenged how I think. They've inspired me. I've learned a huge amount from the conversations I've been lucky enough to have with them. In a few cases, the interaction itself was brief, but they've each had a lasting impact on me.

This list isn't exclusive, nor exhaustive. There are many others doing brilliant work who could have featured in this section. But these are some of the smartest, kindest, most thoughtful minds I've had the pleasure of coming across, who care and think deeply about their work and impact, and show up, inspiring and leading others.

As you read, don't ask: "How do I become them?"

Ask instead: "What can I learn from their experiences?"

And remember that you don't need to have it all figured out to start doing meaningful work.

After you've read this section, look beyond these pages. Reach out to people in your own world. Talk to colleagues, mentors, peers, and the people whose work quietly impresses you. You might find you already know someone worth learning from. You might also realise that parts of *your* journey could help someone else.

Climate and sustainability work isn't a solo pursuit. It's built on community and humanity.

Built through shared learning, mutual support, and the decision to help each other and to figure it out together.

One final note.

I'm lucky to work alongside a huge number of brilliant, fiercely intelligent people, many of whom I would have loved to have featured in this book, and they would have added enormous depth. Many of the people I work alongside and cross paths with in my work deserve a whole chapter or even a book dedicated to the great work they are doing and the positive impact they have on those around them. But I didn't want this section to focus on a single sector (especially since I've probably mentioned heat pumps and the energy sector too many times already). The climate challenge doesn't belong to construction, energy, policy, or tech alone.

It belongs everywhere. And to everyone. Including you.

What follows are some of the people who showed me what that looks like in practice.

These are edited conversations, pulled together from written responses, transcripts, notes, messages, and the occasional hurried coffee. They're not full life stories, just the parts that felt most worth sharing, shaped into something readable and useful, rather than a verbatim transcript of my note-taking skills (which, at times, were questionable).

The conversations that follow exist for one reason: to show that there is no single pathway into climate or sustainability work. Not everyone studied environmental science. Not everyone planned this career. Most people simply noticed something that could be better, and started where they were.

These conversations sit at the heart of this book because seeing how real people arrived here is often far more useful than being told what you *should* do next.

Amy Scarfe - Business Director at Hays Aotearoa

Amy is a Business Director who has worked for Hays for over 15 years, working across the UK, Melbourne, and now Auckland. Hays is a leading global recruitment company, connecting skilled professionals with organisations across a wide range of industries.

Throughout her career, she's recruited for diverse roles in the built environment sector and, in the process, has developed an understanding of the industry and built strong relationships with clients and candidates. In recent years, Amy's focus has shifted towards the environmental and sustainability space, where she recruits for sustainability roles in engineering and construction, ESG, carbon and energy management and climate change.

Q1. What first pulled you into the work you're doing now?

It was a gradual shift as I became increasingly aware of and passionate about the growing importance of sustainability, not just within our company but across the industries we serve. This coincided with a significant rise in demand from clients seeking professionals with expertise in the environment and sustainability, and a global drive within Hays to further support these industries.

Q2. From your perspective at Hays, how has the job market changed?

I have seen a significant change over the years in the job market, with sustainability no longer being a nice-to-have and instead becoming a core part of workforce planning, and both employers and job seekers are aligning their strategies to meet this shift.

On the candidate side, there has been a large increase in people actively seeking climate-aligned roles, and sustainability has become a major consideration for job seekers. The recent Hays Salary Guide identified that sustainability initiatives ranked among the top 12 factors professionals look for beyond salary, and it is a trend that continues to grow in importance.

Upskilling and retraining in sustainability are common themes amongst candidates that I work with, with many investing in courses to develop their skills in this space.

On the employer side, before the recent economic downturn, demand for green skills was rising rapidly across multiple industries. While this momentum slowed over the past year as organisations tightened budgets, conversations with clients suggest a renewed focus on sustainability for 2026. Many businesses are planning to reinvest in sustainability-focused roles, and I think that this area that will regain traction as economic conditions improve.

Q3. Are companies more intentional about environmental values than they used to be?

I frequently have discussions with candidates who are looking to move to a more sustainability-focused role, and the ways in which they can align their technical and soft skills to allow them to do this.

Companies are increasingly positioning their environmental and sustainability values as a core part of their brand internally and externally, and it is often seen as an advantage for attracting and retaining top talent. Many organisations now highlight their sustainability commitments in job descriptions, career pages and during interviews, recognising that candidates want to work for businesses that align with their values.

Q4. What are you working on at the moment that excites you, or what developments in the recruitment market are you most energised by?

I'm excited to see sustainability recruitment conversations slowly gaining momentum again. We're starting to engage with companies about their recruitment plans for 2026, and organisations are again looking to recruit in the environmental and suitability space.

With this anticipated uplift in hiring comes a growing concern around future skills gaps. Clients anticipate skills shortages and are exploring solutions such as skills-based hiring, upskilling programs, and on-the-job training.

Q5. How did you get into the role you are in now? Not everyone follows the same path so it would be great to learn more about yours.

My pivot to sustainability recruitment came through primarily by putting my hand up and demonstrating my passion for this space. It felt like a natural progression, and I could see how important it was becoming for businesses and job seekers, and I wanted to be part of that change. Helping organisations find people who can make a real impact on environmental outcomes is something I'm genuinely excited about, and it's been a big motivator in shaping my role.

Q6. For someone wanting to make a difference — whether they're 18 or 48 — what's one piece of advice you'd offer? Especially if they're wondering how to align their career with climate action.

Network, network, network! Sustainability is a small, close-knit and highly collaborative space in Aotearoa. People are incredibly generous with their time, knowledge, and expertise, and most are happy to connect you with the right opportunities. Start by attending local events, joining professional groups and engaging in online communities.

At the same time, look at the skills you already have that are transferable. Many roles in sustainability need strong communication, project management, data analysis, or stakeholder engagement skills. Then, identify where you need to upskill, for example, taking short courses or volunteering on projects to gain hands-on experience.

Andrew Eagles — Chief Executive, New Zealand Green Building Council

Andrew Eagles is the Chief Executive of the New Zealand Green Building Council. With a background spanning economics, public policy, housing, and construction, his career has taken him from government roles in health policy to senior positions in the UK housing sector and building materials industry. His work overseas strengthened his belief that homes profoundly affect health, well-being, affordability, and climate outcomes. Returning to Aotearoa after 13 years abroad, Andrew now leads NZGBC's mission to transform the built environment, lifting standards, improving the quality of homes and buildings, and driving emissions reduction across the sector.

Q1. What originally drew you toward work that connects policy, people, and sustainability?

My interest began with public policy — how decisions get made, how regulation shapes people's lives, and how systems can be improved. Over time, that curiosity broadened into how buildings influence health, wellbeing, productivity and climate outcomes, and how better standards can improve the lives of thousands of people.

Q2. When did the built environment become central to your thinking about climate and wellbeing?

During my time in the UK, working with housing associations and later leading teams focused on health, reducing running costs, energy efficiency and carbon, I saw how profoundly homes affect people's lives. Good homes support good health, lower emissions, and stronger communities. That's when it clicked: the built environment is one of the strongest levers we have.

Q3. What brought you back to Aotearoa, and why NZGBC?
After 13 years overseas, I wanted to contribute to the future of this whenua — to build something better for tamariki and mokopuna. NZGBC offered the opportunity to help transform an entire sector toward healthier, more cost-effective, low-emissions homes and buildings.

Q4. For readers new to NZGBC, how would you describe what the organisation does today?
We're a purpose-led not-for-profit providing the tools and standards that define what good looks like in buildings — Homestar, Green Star, NABERSNZ, HomeFit — and supporting the sector to deliver healthier, efficient, lower-carbon homes and buildings. We also advocate for change and collaborate globally with 78 other Green Building Councils.

Q5. What personal qualities or mindsets have helped you most in this work?
Resilience, collaboration, and listening. Real change takes time, and partnership is essential. Listening to clients, colleagues, and communities builds trust — and leads to better outcomes than simply telling people what to do.

Q6. What advice would you give to someone wanting to build a purpose-driven career in sustainability or the built environment?

There's no single pathway. We need people from policy, engineering, architecture, science, IT, communications — everything. Get exposure to real projects. Learn how homes and buildings actually function. And remember that this challenge will reshape every part of the economy, so every skillset has a place.

Q7. Any books, podcasts or resources that have influenced your thinking?

- *Five Times Faster* — Simon Sharpe
- *Cleaning Up (Podcast)* — Michael Liebreich
- *Let Me Sum Up* (Podcast) — Luke Menzel, Fran Muskovic, Peta Credlin, etc.
- RNZ's *Nine to Noon* political commentary
  Understanding climate isn't just about science, it's about politics, history, economics, and human decision-making.

Andy O'Hare — Senior Advisor, Centre for Sustainable Finance: Toitū Tahua

Andy is a banking professional with the majority of his career spent in London within the Commercial & Institutional division of the major UK bank, NatWest. He has held senior leadership roles spanning Pricing and Capital Management, Climate, and Energy sectors. After leaving banking—and relocating from the UK—in late 2024, Andy joined the Centre for Sustainable Finance: Toitū Tahua in Auckland in 2025 as a Senior Advisor. In this role, he draws on his banking expertise to work with the finance and energy sectors, as well as the New Zealand Government, to develop novel financing solutions that support the delivery of abundant, affordable, clean energy for all in New Zealand.

Q1. Your career journey spans traditional finance, energy, and sustainability, can you walk us through that transition and what inspired each shift?

I was in banking ever since leaving university. It wasn't an industry that I'd particularly targeted but once I'd landed in a bank I felt pretty comfortable as numbers, maths etc. always came to me quite easily. Long story short, in around 2020 I led pricing strategy for all business and commercial debt, and this also included some capital allocation strategy activity - which is effectively utilising pricing and pricing models to deploy capital more heavily into certain types of businesses, sectors etc. than others. At that time, NatWest had become one of the most "progressive" banks from a Climate strategy perspective. I think we were the biggest bank globally to have a published transition plan, and STBI approved targets. Not only did this mean I was indirectly exposed to "Climate" as it started to run through most bank activities, but our capital allocation strategy needed to align to those bank climate targets. So we started to review and evolve pricing and capital allocation strategy in this context. I became pretty interested in the climate challenge and because I'd built up a decent amount of credibility within the bank, when the Commercial Bank needed a Head of Climate for a short(ish) term secondment, I put my hat in the ring and was asked to do it. It was great because I'd gone from being very technical and specialised into something much broader. The climate role essentially focused on how we balance our climate objectives (ambitiously reducing financed emissions) with our BAU commercial objectives (balance sheet growth, profitability targets etc.).

Being honest, that move was as much about getting out of my previous job as I'd been in it for 4 years and needed a change, but the move from Climate to Energy that came 18 months or so later was more considered. I loved the Climate gig, but I had developed a particular interest in the transport / energy space, rather than (for example) agriculture. So, when the role in energy came up, I jumped at it. My title was Head of Natural Resources, Renewables & Utilities. It was super interesting as I covered oil & gas, as well as renewables and newer tech (hydrogen, CCS etc.). I always liked my pricing job, but I was never overly interested in the subject. I never used to read pricing books in my spare time! Whereas I now spend lots of time reading up on energy and find it fascinating. More than anything it's the economics of energy, and of the energy transition. So it's been great to land in a job in New Zealand that has a big energy focus, but let's me leverage my banking background.

Q2. You've worked in both the UK and now in Aotearoa New Zealand. How have those different contexts influenced your perspective on the work you do? What similarities or differences have stood out to you?

It's quite a difficult one for me to answer, because my UK work life was almost solely within a huge corporate bank, and my NZ comparison is a very small not-for-profit. So it's hard to know what is driven by being at the other end of the entity size spectrum, rather than a UK / NZ difference. Something I've noticed is the ability to make a tangible difference in NZ vs. the UK. Everything feels more achievable and accessible which is largely down to economy / country size. I guess it's just a case of fewer layers between any given person and key decision makers which increases the ability to influence. I think this provides an incentive to be ambitious. Things in the UK probably were achievable, but maybe didn't seem it. It seems less farfetched here that you can be a driver of significant change and so it possibly lowers a psychological barrier.

From a sustainability perspective I'd say you largely have the same tensions and dynamics at play. The argument has somewhat shifted from an environmental one to an economic / resilience / independance one. It's similarly politicised though.

Q3. Sustainable finance is a term that's gaining traction, but what does it mean to you in practice?

For me Sustainable Finance is a term that's in some ways a bit of a red herring. If you set aside true philanthropy, then finance is about economics. Leaning on my experience, if you think about bank lending and pricing, sustainable finance can often be cheaper than normal finance, but this needs to be economically logical. A simple example is car manufacturers. If you lend to a European car manufacturer that has no plans to develop an EV range, despite wide ranging EV mandates in the markets you sell into, then you should account for the heightened credit risk that that counterparty carries, noting the likely shrinking total addressable market for their products. The "sustainable finance" that you provide to car manufacturers that **do** develop EV ranges should be at a lower interest rate (all else being equal) to reflect the enhanced credit quality vs. those without credible transition (and as such business) plans. This is how finance has always worked. I don't see non-economically driven sustainable finance as being sustainable from a scalability perspective.

The settings have to be such that the sustainable option is the economically preferable option. Rather than hoping that finance can be used to incentivise the economically subordinate option.

Q4. What advice would you give to someone at the start of their career who might be looking to work in sustainability?

I'd probably say, look to get into a role / industry that interests you regardless of the sustainability element, because the sustainability element is something you can bring. Whether that's architectural design, cars, or even banking. You can bring the sustainability focus to that place of work, so if you can combine sustainability with another interest, that feels like a good place to be in.

Q5. Looking ahead, what are you most optimistic about, in sustainable finance, the energy transition, or the way capital markets are evolving to respond to climate challenges?

The economics of the energy transition is what makes me most optimistic. The cost reductions observed across solar and batteries in recent years are astonishing. Not only is the tech becoming cheaper, performance is also improving. I'm a strong believer that focus should be placed on mass deployment of the low-cost, readily available tech that will get us 80-90% of the way to net zero, rather than the harder technological advancements required for that last 10-20%. Being a numbers person, the flexibility of batteries, and how BESS business models vary across geographies and energy markets is fascinating. They will have a huge part to play in accelerating towards net zero.

Anje de Jager – Founder of Saudade Marketing

Anje founded Saudade Marketing, a B2B content and positioning agency for sustainability-driven companies. She works with consultancies, SaaS businesses, and climate tech founders who need their marketing to match the ambition of their impact.

She didn't start here. After studying international business and briefly chasing roles at multinationals, travel shifted her perspective. She realised conserving the world's beauty mattered more than climbing corporate ladders. A pivot into a "sustainability-driven" SaaS startup felt right—until she saw they were more interested in growth than impact, targeting the very companies she'd walked away from.

A chance office move changed everything. A sustainability consultancy moved in next door. Anje got to know the team, mentioned she'd love to work somewhere like that, and talked the CEO into letting her kickstart their content marketing on the side. Six months later, she went full-time. She's been at the intersection of marketing and sustainability ever since— translating complex topics like CSRD and ESG into clear, credible narratives, and challenging founders to choose substance over polish.

Q1. Can you share a bit about your career journey so far and how you found your way into climate communication and storytelling? Was this something you always planned, or did it evolve over time?

I definitely didn't plan for it—but that's also what your 20s are for, I guess. I studied international business, convinced I'd end up at a multinational like P&G or Shell, chasing the big bucks (a narrative I'd copied from my parents). Then travel opened my eyes. I realised I needed more of a purpose than a paycheck, and that working for those companies wasn't going to help conserve the world's beauty—it would undermine it.

I pivoted into a "sustainability-driven" SaaS startup, but they were more interested in growth than impact, ironically targeting the exact companies I'd walked away from. A chance office move changed everything: a sustainability consultancy moved in next door. I got to know the team, mentioned I'd love to work somewhere like that, and talked the CEO into letting me kickstart their content marketing on the side. Six months later, I went full-time.

After leaving the consultancy, I spent a year at a freelance matchmaking platform for sustainability—like Fiverr, but greener. It was fun, but I missed being hands-on with clients. So I came back to my original focus. I'm still looking for other ways to make an impact in this space. Marketing is a skill I have; sustainability is something I'm passionate about. I'm sure I'll combine the two in different ways.

Q2. You speak about the importance of communication in climate work. Why do you think storytelling, language, and framing matter so much in this space, and what do you think the climate movement has historically done well (and not so well) when it comes to how we communicate?

Storytelling matters because it has the power to reconnect us with the planet, with nature, and with each other. People always say "awareness is the first step," but I've learned that awareness rarely changes behaviour on its own. What can shift things is a story that sparks something—a feeling, a question, a realisation that sticks.

Historically, I think the climate movement has been too isolated and a bit exclusive. When I first started eating vegan, for example, it came with so much pressure to be perfect. But the world doesn't need 100 perfect vegans—it needs millions of people reducing their meat and dairy intake. The movement has sometimes made people feel like they're either all in or they don't belong, which shuts out the very people we need.

What I'd love to see is a communications effort—and a lobby movement—that rivals the oil and gas industry. They've mastered storytelling and influence. We need to match that, but with honesty, accessibility, and a message that invites people in rather than pushing them away.

Q3. What have been some of the biggest challenges you've faced working in this space, whether that's navigating overwhelm, scepticism, burnout, or trying to cut through the noise? How have you learned to handle them?

Navigating overwhelm has been a big one these past few years. The news is rarely positive, and because I care so deeply, it started to affect my mental health. I've learned to create boundaries and focus mainly on the things I do control—but that doesn't mean it doesn't still get to me sometimes.

I've also had to learn to cut through the noise. A lot of the sustainability movement has gotten too caught up in reporting, compliance, and box-ticking. It feels like a distraction from the real problem. We're not going to fix this mess with "business as usual" practices, even if they're slightly greener. That's a tough reality because it questions parts of the sustainability profession itself—but I think the better we're able to challenge the system rather than just its practices, the more impact we'll make.

Systems thinking was a big revelation for me. It helped me zoom out and see where the real leverage points are. It doesn't make the work easier, but it does make it clearer.

4. What strengths or skills do you think you bring to this work? Are there qualities you now recognise as valuable that didn't originally feel "climate-related"?

Critical thinking and questioning information have been surprisingly valuable. I didn't realize how much the sustainability space would need that—the ability to push back on greenwashing, challenge narratives, and cut through the noise of performative action.

Ironically, my commercial thinking has also been a huge asset. I've worked with founders who are sustainability experts and incredibly passionate, but they struggle to gain visibility. They know their stuff inside out, but translating that into clear positioning, compelling messaging, and actual market traction? That's where I come in. I didn't know there was space for that kind of thinking in the climate movement—I was convinced you needed a relevant degree or a background in environmental science to work here.

Thank heaven that wasn't the case. What I've learned is that the movement needs all kinds of skills: strategists, communicators, marketers, systems thinkers. The climate crisis is too big and too complex for any one discipline to solve. We need people who can bridge gaps, and that's exactly what I do.

5. For someone reading this who cares about climate but doesn't see themselves as a scientist or policy expert, what advice would you give, especially to those interested in communication, media, creative work, or storytelling?

It's such a cliché, but it's a cliché for a reason: just do it. I promise you'll be more fulfilled. There's something deeply satisfying about being part of the solution, even in small ways.

A lot of people think they don't have anything meaningful to contribute to the climate movement, but I'm here to tell you that you do. The movement desperately needs people with communication skills, creative thinking, and passion. You don't need to be a scientist or a policy expert or even a sustainability expert—you just need a willingness to learn. And guess what? That becomes a whole lot easier when you're actually interested.

Start where you are. Look at the work you're already doing and ask how it could serve the climate. Can you tell better stories? Build stronger brands for the right companies? Challenge the narratives that keep us stuck? Your skills matter. The movement is bigger than any one discipline, and right now, we need storytellers, marketers, and communicators just as much as we need scientists. Maybe more.

Charlotte McKeon - Teacher in Charge of Trades, One Tree Hill College.

Charlotte McKeon is the Teacher in Charge of Trades at One Tree Hill College. In addition to teaching Trade, she works in collaboration with the school and community to provide real-world training opportunities for students pursuing careers in Trades. Most recently, with the support of her LBP Builder, her Level 3 BCITO students renovated an ex-Kainga Ora 1970s end-of-life house into a Homestar level 7 house. Charlotte is currently completing her Master's of Architecture degree at the University of Auckland. She lives with her husband, two teenagers and a black miniature schnauzer dog named Betty.

Q1. You've been involved in some incredible real-world building projects with students, including the One Tree Hill Trades College home renovation. Can you tell us about this project, what you were trying to achieve, and what impact you've seen on the students involved?

We have been very fortunate to receive significant community support for our Trade program. In 2022, we converted our carpentry class into a Trade Academy because the projects the students were undertaking were not challenging enough. In our local community, houses were being cleared to make way for densified living, thus we saw an opportunity to renovate an existing end-of-life home. Our LBP Builder on staff is a firm believer that there is a lot to be learnt working on an old home. Especially important are the problem-solving skills and the ability to communicate clearly.

Our objective was to better prepare our students for transitioning from school into a trade apprenticeship. They may have knowledge and experience with tools, but they must also know how to communicate in the workplace. In order to support adulting, we introduced a mentoring program called RAP in partnership with our local Rotary club. We purchased an end of life house for $1.00 from Kainga Ora who moved it to the school. We fenced off the house and set it up as an independent worksite, assigning the LBP Builder to run the job, and provided daily opportunities for students to work with a variety of qualified tradies, thus exposing them to authentic workplace experiences and skill development.

The transformation we have seen is incredible. Before the house, our students would not look at or speak with unknown adults confidently. When we sent students out on a work placement, they would not show up if they had had to drop a sibling to school before work. Today, our students' success in transitioning to trade apprenticeships is attributed to both the mentoring program and working on the house. Our students communicate challenges with much less hesitation. They communicate with greater confidence because they have practiced repeatedly working collaboratively on the house project. They understand building concepts because they have done the work. Our students opt to join us on Saturdays and during school holidays to expand on their learning. They are keen to learn and experience different trades, speak to tradies and grow their own knowledge and experience.

Q2. Your own learning journey spans architecture, hands-on building experience, and education. How did your career

path evolve, and what moments helped shape the direction you're on today?

I started out as a structural welder in the 90's and went on to become a Metalwork Teacher at Penrose High. There were not many opportunities for women then. I left NZ in 2000 and went to study and work in design overseas. I returned to New Zealand in 2016. Out of the blue, a One Tree Hill College (previously, Penrose High School) staff member from the 90's heard I was in town and asked if I would come in and help out. The school was short-staffed in Technology. Metal work was essentially obsolete; all the welders, lathes and foundry were gone. I started doing small wood projects based on my design background and brought in an LBP builder to support and upskill me. This grew yearly. When Covid shut us down, I had time to reflect and consider my next move. I knew I wanted more challenge at age 45. I considered becoming a qualified builder until a BCITO person told me, "It's not great to be on a roof at 50+ years of age." Thus, I applied for the Bachelor of Architecture program at Auckland University. However, I was completely unaware that one couldn't take the course part-time. I am now in the final 6 months of the Master of Architecture program and it has been an absolute privilege. I feel extremely fortunate to have attended inspiring lectures and been exposed to a variety of people, movements and concepts. Admittedly, it is a lot of juggling with a full-time job, full-time study and two teenagers, but absolutely worth it. My studies introduced me to Homestar and The New Zealand Green Building Council, and that learning has only continued to expand.

Q3. What is your "why"? What personally motivates you to do this work, and what keeps you showing up for these students and projects day after day?

Because, if you can do better, why wouldn't you? I can do better in my role as a teacher. My students can do better as learners experiencing trade. There is no limit to what we can do. I want the students to see and experience the opportunities that are available, and if not, then maybe they need to create those opportunities. I show up because I love the challenge of taking nothing and making it into something. It is rewarding to see the students take ownership and create their own careers. It is a privilege to be supported by an incredibly generous and visionary community. There are so many, many people involved in the success of this program, and every piece matters. We all want the very best for our students, and we are doing it together.

Q4. Many of your projects naturally align with sustainability principles, from energy efficiency to material reuse to community impact. How do you think hands-on construction education can contribute to both environmental and social outcomes?

I believe that if you know better, you can do better. We only know what we know. If our students are learning to build beyond code, if they understand what a tight thermal envelope is and how air most commonly leaks out of a house, they know based on personal experience why that is not desirable. We all want to be warm, dry and not have health issues. Students experience how to build without leaks by taping joints and cutting accurately. These simple practices can make a big difference. Students cut and fit the insulation to size. They know it has to be snug but not squished and not loose or baggy. These are conversations that are had when on the tools doing the mahi. It makes sense to take a bit more time and do it right because someone's family is going to live in this house over the next 50 years.

Q5. For young people who might be unsure about traditional academic pathways, or who are curious about careers in trades, design, or sustainable building, what advice would you give them?

Have a go! We are fortunate to have a number of Trade Academies in NZ schools: BCITO, ETCO, MITO, Connexus all work with schools to offer 10 week work placements for 16+ year olds and we have supporting programs like ARA which provide opportunities for students to be on a controlled building site. Ask your school's Careers Department. If you don't get an answer you like, go to BCITO or another provider and ask for suggestions. Keep asking until you get an answer that gives you an opportunity to have an experience.

There are so many pathways, academic and practical. Students can do both. We don't need to pick one or the other. No one is born knowing how to do any of these Trades. We all have to learn. Find good people who support you in your pathway of interest. They are out there!

Dan Smith — National ESG Manager, SHAPE Australia

Dan Smith is the ESG Manager at SHAPE Australia. With a background spanning project coordination, sustainability strategy, and the built environment, his career has taken him from the UK HVAC sector to leading ESG delivery across construction and fit-out projects in Australia. Dan's experience building a sustainability function within a global Japanese corporate shaped his belief that sustainability only works when it is practical, commercially grounded, and owned across the business. His work focuses on translating complex sustainability challenges into clear, actionable strategies that connect purpose with performance.

Now based in Australia, Dan supports SHAPE's mission to deliver meaningful environmental and social value through sustainable retrofit and fit-out, helping the built environment play a constructive role in addressing climate change.

Q1. Your pathway into construction and sustainability wasn't exactly traditional. How did it all begin?

My journey didn't follow the "usual" pathway — if such a thing exists. I started out in recruitment after a 2.5-year working holiday through Australia, New Zealand, Fiji, and the Philippines. That short stint was a crucial catalyst; it showed me more clearly what I *didn't* want than what I did. An application for a Project Coordinator role at Mitsubishi Electric Living Environmental Systems followed, and that was the beginning of my interest in the built environment and, eventually, sustainability.

Q2. What drew you towards sustainability, and when did it start to become central to your work?

There was no single eureka moment — just a gradual pull. Experiencing the places most affected by climate change sparked a desire to give something back. At Mitsubishi, my role evolved, but one theme kept guiding me: sustainability. Decarbonisation, circularity, social value, carbon accounting, reporting, education — the list grew as my curiosity grew. Through upskilling, countless seminars and courses (including Sustainable Business Management at Cambridge Institute for Sustainability Leadership), and the support of a great mentor, Chris Newman, I eventually became National Sustainability & Construction Manager.

Q3. Along your journey, who have been the role models or mentors who shaped your approach and leadership style?

I've been incredibly fortunate with the people around me.

- Chris Newman, the unsung hero of sustainability, taught me how to distill complexity into simple, actionable insights.
- Jen Kelly, Head of Sustainability at Chester Zoo, showed me the power of relationship-driven collaboration.
- Scott McKay demonstrated what strong, people-centred leadership looks like and how to have a confident voice at the top table.

Q4. What motivates you now — is it climate impact, opportunity, or something else?

My motivation today is rooted in the same spark that first pulled me in: a deep appreciation for nature and the beauty we're at risk of losing. I believe my greatest impact comes from working in sustainability in the built environment — advocating for spaces where we live, work, and play that harmonise with ecosystems rather than compete with them.

Q5. You've now crossed continents — how did the move to Australia shape your career, and what does your role look like today?

After 3.5 exciting years building what was essentially a start-up, revenue-generating sustainability function within a global Japanese corporate, a sliding-doors moment opened the opportunity to continue my career in Australia. I'm now the National ESG Manager at SHAPE, a national fit-out and construction specialist leading the way in sustainable retrofit. It's a new landscape and a new way of working, but still guided by the same core theme: sustainability.

Q6. Any books or films that have influenced your thinking on leadership or environmental stewardship?

Two stand out:

- **Book:** *Legacy* by James Kerr — inspired by the All Blacks; a reminder that *"society grows great when old men plant trees whose shade they will never see."*

- **Film: *The Biggest Little Farm*** — a beautiful example of what's possible when we embrace environmental stewardship and work with nature rather than against it.

Emily Mabin Sutton - Independent Director at Clean Planet, Chief Executive of Climate Club NZ.

Emily Mabin Sutton is a climate action leader and co-founder of Climate Club Aotearoa, working with organisations and communities to turn climate awareness into practical action. With a background spanning software and technology, product management and global tech startups, she brings a systems-focused and human-centred approach to sustainability. Emily facilitates Climate training workshops and works with businesses, councils and leadership teams to build climate literacy and confidence. She also serves as a trustee and associate trustee across several organisations, including the Cool-Safe Trust, contributing to governance and sector leadership. Emily is passionate about making climate action accessible, inclusive and embedded in everyday decision-making.

Q1. Your journey spans biotechnology, product management, founding companies and charities, working in both Lisbon and New Zealand, what's the thread that connects all those experiences?

There is no common thread when you look at it that way! I believe in "The Squiggly Line", Claudia Batten's concept. The path to what you want to do isn't always linear. I've always dreamed of running my own impact organisation and working to create impact, and over the last 10 years I've been trying to figure out how to achieve that. I had hypothesised that software could be a way to affect global change. But as I started working in software more, I began to realise that not all software is changing the world for good, and many technologies are harmful and have global impacts that aren't imagined when they are created. One day, I quit my job and started to run climate workshops and learnt as much as I could about problems I genuinely wanted to solve. And now I'm fortunate enough to spend my time working in teams with talented people, solving problems that really matter, like climate change and consumer rights issues.

Q2. What made you decide to start your own companies or organisations, rather than follow a traditional career path, and what was the driving mission behind those ventures?

50 years ago, the world of work was a more stable, predictable place. And one job could last your whole lifetime. You could have a career in a legal firm, but with the pace of technological change, jobs are changing really fast and whole fields are being created or automated. And I'm not entirely sure that a traditional career will be one job with one skill set. But also, I like to learn and grow, and I'm curious about a variety of different parts of the business. So, in one field or function, I felt limited or unnecessarily nosy. It was scary taking the leap to start my own company and charity. So, I started with consulting. I was part time consulting and part time starting my climate initiatives. But equally, I knew I would regret it if I didn't because it felt like the most impactful way I could spend my time. So, for a long time, I worked without very much pay, so I was also privileged to be able to consult and work without that

much pay and then eventually I was able to do this work full time.

Q3. How has your background in startup shaped the way you approach sustainability, community engagement or climate action?

My favourite part about being inside startups is that you're allowed to make mistakes - it's called learning - and I now bring that mindset of being agile and data oriented and pragmatic, and outcome oriented, has meant that our ways of operating mirror that. It's helped us stay focused on the activities that create the most results and build a very low margin, all money spent on important things type of organisation. So not talking or doing.

Q4. As a relatively young director, founder and leader of multiple organisations, how do you balance vision, leadership, and the practical demands of running organisations?

I believe wholeheartedly that whoever is delivering the task for a project is the most likely the best decision maker on that project. Having awesome teams, teams of people who are able to run within entire projects and own their work. I'm really lucky to now have wonderful epic team members who are able to run with entire projects. And by aligning on the key outcomes of goals of a project, they can learn and try different things with my support, but equally trusted to be able to experiment and plan as they would like. I think it's a high trust environment while being results driven. And I really personally thrive off variety and learning from multiple organisations and being able to provide input into multiple organisation strategies is incredibly helpful and insightful. So being able to bring learnings from each of the different realms of organisations that seem to add value where they're applied as well.

Q5. What do you see as the biggest opportunities — and biggest challenges — for community, education and climate engagement in New Zealand (or globally) right now?

In communities it's incredibly hard just to create behaviour change and to get people involved. It's incredibly hard to justify and try and change the way that people see the world and the need for money or the time and imperative for change. Any time you're trying to change someone's behaviour, they need to see what's in it for them as well as what's in it for the planet. I think it's a wonderful space to work in. It's really fun, and you have so many genuinely inspiring conversations, and there's so much work that is done in this space that is unpaid. It's frustrating that our worldview doesn't value this type of work as paid work as much as it could.

Q6. Looking back on everything you've done so far, what advice would you give someone starting out today who wants to build a purpose-driven career across business, social impact and sustainability?

I actually think that there's no reason to get skills and learn somewhere else. If you're passionate about something, just start doing it as soon as you like because what I'm learning from now running an organisation is I have learned some useful people management and project management skills in my career software, but equally a lot of the job is learning as you go. And I think any new initiative can be hampered by the traits that you learn as well as the traits that you need to unlearn. If you have the passion, don't wait, just do it. Go and find all the people who are doing something similar at work in the space and build your community, build your board of advisors, build your community of people who can help mentor you and who will welcome you into the space.

Q7. What's a moment of failure, doubt, or unravelling that ended up shaping you as a founder and leader?

I think for a long time I didn't feel like I had enough knowledge to work in climate, actually. When I really wanted to work on a problem, I was super passionate about, but I didn't feel confident or like I knew enough about the area, and that stopped me for a long time from moving industries. Then I did the Climate Fresk workshop, and it showed me the whole picture of everything. I realised that it's a really helpful tool that gives you the confidence to be able to actually say, I know enough and learn on the job and you can see the big picture and therefore see that you don't need to know all of the technical details about every area to understand the general systems of what's happening and what's causing climate change and what we can do about it. And so I think the concepts that we're all learning, and I don't know that much, and staying humble shapes me as a founder because I never assumed to know. I would hope that I never assumed to know all the answers, but I like asking interesting questions and having interesting conversations and getting the right people together to have that discussion. I also try to deliberately be welcoming and nonjudgmental of people who don't know that much about climate change because even though you don't know much about one thing, you might know a lot about data engineering or behaviour change, which is all very helpful when it comes to persuading people to change the way they behave.

Q8. Are there any books, films, podcasts or thinkers that have influenced your worldview, leadership style, or approach to climate and community work?

- Anything by Jason Hickel is awesome.
- Slowing the Sun by Nadine Hura
- This Changes Everything: Capitalism vs. the Climate by Naomi Klein
- Narratives for Change by The Workshop

Esther Evening – Sustainability & Strategy Analyst at Mercury, Global Future Energy Leader at World Energy Council.

A young energy leader shaping climate strategy — proving there is no single pathway into purpose-led work and that curiosity can outrun credentials. Esther Evening works at the intersection of energy, sustainability, and long-term strategy. Currently a Sustainability and Strategy Analyst at Mercury NZ, she supports thinking around the energy transition and how climate considerations are embedded into future decision-making. Recognised as a Future Energy Leader with the World Energy Council, Esther brings a thoughtful, systems-focused perspective to climate and energy challenges, with a strong emphasis on inclusion, learning, and creating space for the next generation to help shape the future.

Q1. At 17, who has a 10-year plan? How did your career journey begin, and what guided your early choices?
At 17, I genuinely had no idea what direction to take. I applied for a Bachelor of Commerce, Bachelor of Science (Food) and a Bachelor of Nursing — three completely unrelated options. My parents didn't go to university (Mum went later in life), so I didn't feel pressured into a specific pathway. In the end, I chose not to go to university at all.

I've always lived by a simple idea: "do more good than bad." I didn't chase a job title — I chased values. I wanted to find an organisation whose values aligned with mine. That's how I discovered the energy sector — and Mercury. Their values clicked, so I applied and started in customer service while working part-time at a café.

From the beginning, curiosity was my biggest accelerator. I constantly asked "why?" Why do we do this? Why hasn't this changed? That mindset helped me move into customer risk, then process improvement, simply by following the questions.

Q2. Your growth has been rapid. What opened doors for you, and how did you enter the sustainability and climate space?
A few years into Mercury, I joined the Young Energy Professionals Network (YEPN) — and it changed everything. Suddenly, I was exposed to the whole energy sector, not just my organisation. YEPN eventually asked me to join the board and then become Co-Chair. Saying yes before I felt ready became a pattern and honestly, it's the reason so many doors opened for me.

Through YEPN's mentor coffee programme, I met someone in Mercury's sustainability team. He became a mentor and involved me in research projects, which sparked my interest in the sustainability side of energy.

I reached out to Mercury's then Chief Sustainability Officer, Lucie, to understand her team and the steps I'd need to move into that space. Soon after, an opportunity to join the team came up and I joined the sustainability team, working on climate strategy with a focus on scenario planning and disclosures. This is the "big picture" work: the what-ifs of the future, and how our decisions today shape tomorrow. It suits me, I like living in the space between detail and possibility.

Q3. You chose not to go to university. How has that shaped your path, and what have you learned from taking an alternative route?
I don't regret skipping university for a second. People assume skipping university closes doors. For me, it opened them sooner. While many of my peers were in their first year of lectures, I already had full-time work, real experience, and—honestly—a three-year head start. I also avoided the student debt that holds so many people back.

There are careers where degrees are essential. But in many others, what matters is your willingness to learn, speak up, ask questions, and take opportunities. University teaches you how to learn, but if you naturally know how to do that — or if you get thrown into research-heavy projects early — you can leap-frog the whole system.

Climate work reinforces this, too. It's vast and complex, so I focus on the day-to-day: what action can I take today that makes tomorrow easier? A single choice, influence, or conversation can ripple out to hundreds or even thousands of people over time. That's what keeps me focused.

Q4. You've become a leader in your field at a young age. What has that been like — imposter syndrome, speaking up,

mentoring others?

I'm an overthinker, and I do struggle with imposter syndrome, but when an opportunity comes to speak on a stage, sit on a panel, or contribute to something meaningful — I take it. If you want to have a positive impact, you have to put yourself out there. I've learned that impact happens on the other side of discomfort.

After seven years at Mercury, I've become an expert in my own right: shaping climate strategy, challenging processes, assessing long-term risks, and navigating both technical and people-focused challenges. I've learned the value of using my voice.

"Be what you can see."
I've also shifted from mentee to mentor. I still seek guidance — every day is a learning day — but I now support others too. My advice to anyone wanting to enter the sustainability or energy space?
Talk to someone you admire, and talk to someone you don't. Different perspectives challenge assumptions and help you grow.

Q5. Your role as a Global Future Energy Leader sounds exciting — can you tell us about that experience and how it has shaped your thinking?

Becoming a Global Future Energy Leader still feels surreal. It's a network of emerging leaders from across the world, all working on completely different parts of the energy system but facing the same challenges: the energy trilemma, the pace of technology, climate urgency, affordability, equity — and the human side of all of it.

What I've gained most so far is perspective. Aotearoa's energy system is genuinely world-leading in places, but we also underestimate how much our experience can help other countries. Sharing our wins, and our failures, has been valuable.

Being in global conversations has also strengthened the way I approach scenario planning and climate strategy at home. When you hear what keeps people in other countries up at night, you start to see your own system differently. It pushes you to think longer-term, and more creatively, about resilience and opportunity.

But honestly, the network itself is the biggest gift. Having people from Panama, Australia, Finland, Uruguay, Chile and elsewhere challenge your thinking is humbling in the best way. It reminds you that energy transitions are, at their core, human transitions.

Q6. Finally, are there any books, films, podcasts, or other resources that have shaped the way you think about energy, climate, or purpose?

An idea that's shaped my thinking lately is Mel Robbins' Let Them philosophy. It's a reminder to stop trying to control things you can't, let people make their own decisions, let situations unfold and instead focus energy on the positive change you can drive. That mindset has kept me grounded in climate work, where it's so easy to feel responsible for everything all at once.

Graham Hendra – Heat Pump Development Engineer at Haier Europe

Hi, my name's Graham. I work for a Chinese electronics giant in R&D, trying to help my developers make heat pumps simpler, easier and friendlier. I've spent the last 15 years working in heat pumps, mostly selling them to plumbers and heating engineers through a distribution / wholesale company, which I started with 2 friends.

When I started in heat pumps, the industry was very small, so it was easy to become an expert and a bit of an industry leader, it's a role I sort of fell into. During COVID, I decided I was so fed up with explaining the same things about heat pumps 20 times a day that I thought I would start blogging on LinkedIn and wrote a simple guide to heat pumps. IT didn't work. Now I'm "famous" in the very loosest of ways, I get more questions than ever before.

Before heat pumps, I spent 20 years in air conditioning, starting as an engineer, progressing to after-sales support and finally running the UK division of a Korean electronics giant.

Q1. What first pulled you into this work, was it one moment or a gradual realisation?

I got into heat pumps because I hated my job, I was miserable at work, my boss was an idiot. I went to a trade dinner and someone I knew (Niel Afram) asked me why I was so sad. I told him I wanted out and he offered me a job in heat pumps; they are just air conditioning systems that heat so I knew a bit about the tech. I took the job, so I'm here because I didn't like my job, pure luck.

Q2. What part of your journey so far — experience, mindset, even mistakes — has helped you most in doing what you do now?

I'm a curious person, I like to know how things work, I love taking things to bits and learning the processes inside. This lead me to being a curious engineer who found it agony if I couldn't understand why I couldn't fix anything. It's an illness all good engineers have. That compounded with the fact that I have a massive ego problem and I'm never satisfied led me to my current role in R and D. I don't think our technology is very good, it's not cutting edge and I don't think the designers of the equipment are doing a very good job. So, when I was asked if I thought I could make heat pumps or more specifically the company I work for heat pump better I said yes.

Q3. What are you working on right now that excites you, or what's coming next that you're proud of?

I'm working on a thermostat for the home that normal humans can operate. Think heating controls in a car, a car is the most sophisticated heating system you will ever come across, and anyone can operate it without a manual. Now think of the last hotel you were in, could you use the controls of the heating? I couldn't. I'm just trying to make heating controls in the house as easy to use as they are in a car. In our industry that is really groundbreaking.

Q4. Climate work can be incredibly rewarding but also exhausting. How do you stay motivated or grounded?

If I'm honest, I don't think of my job as having anything to do with Climate. I know that by Ryan's measure, I have a dark Green Job, I help produce hardware which has a very significant impact on a home's carbon intensity. But I don't feel I should take any credit for this carbon saving. If I don't make something good, you won't buy it, and the impact will be zero. I sort of feel like I'm helping the climate by accident.

Q5. For someone wanting to make a difference, whether they're 18 or 48, what's one piece of advice you'd offer?

Only do things you are passionate about. If you want to change the impact you, your friends or your company make, then get on with it. Don't be a wet lettuce about it, grab the opportunity by the horns and make a bloody difference. If your heart's not in it, do something else, even if it is working in a coal-fired power station.

Q6. Finally, are there any books, films, podcasts, or other resources that have shaped the way you think about energy, climate, or purpose?

My favourite film is Predator, but it's a stretch to claim it's about climate change.

But when it comes to books, *Sustainable Energy - without the hot air* - by David MacKay is the best book on climate and energy ever written. It's a true masterpiece. It's written in 2 ways: simple for idiots and politicians, and complex for scientists and educated readers. So, anyone can access it. It helps you understand the enormity of the task, including the numbers you will need.

Jodi McLaren – Technical Lead, Sustainability at Mainfreight Group

I'm a young professional working in sustainability within the freight industry, helping create solutions that reduce environmental impact. Outside of work, I'm happiest exploring nature - whether it's beaches, forests, or mountains- and travelling to experience new cultures and landscapes. I also enjoy sports, reading, and the occasional board game or pub quiz. Life for me is about balance: staying active, learning, and appreciating the beauty of our planet. Driven by a passion for sustainability and a love for the outdoors, I aim to make a positive impact every day.

Q1. To start us off, can you tell us a bit about your current role in the logistics sector and what you're responsible for day to day?

I'm the Mainfreight Group Technical Lead for our Sustainability Team, responsible for developing and implementing tools and processes that track sustainability metrics across our operations and for our customers.

On the day to day, this can mean I'm working on anything from writing software specifications, testing systems or designing Power BI dashboards to facilitating customer discussions, running team workshops or analysing climate-related risks. A major part of my role involves compiling our Group-wide greenhouse gas inventory, which helps us understand our emissions footprint and identify the most efficient strategies for reduction.

Q2. Logistics is often invisible to most people, but it underpins almost everything we rely on. What impact do you see your role and your company having on businesses, communities, and the environment?

Logistics often goes unnoticed because when it works well, goods arrive on time and in perfect condition – so it can be easy to overlook the effort involved in that process. Yet everything from raw materials to finished products rely on logistics services.

My role helps make the sustainability impact of these movements visible. By working with customers to help them understand the sustainability impact of their logistics choices, we enable smarter decisions. These decisions can have flow-on effects. Lower emissions transport modes can improve air quality and better packaging can reduce waste - benefiting not just the business itself, but also the communities and environment they operate in.

Q3. How did you find your way into logistics and into the sustainability role you're in now? Was it planned, or did it evolve over time?

At university, I learned about New Zealand's heavy reliance on oil for energy, despite our highly renewable electricity grid. This motivated me to join a freight company where I could influence the transition to lower emissions fuels.

When I first joined, sustainability was only just emerging as a focus. I helped with our first greenhouse gas inventory audit and developed the initial emissions tracking tools.

Today, we have sustainability team members around the world, working not only on emissions, but also climate-related risks, customer decarbonisation projects and broader sustainability reporting requirements. We also empower branches to implement their own sustainability initiatives and share their successes across the network so they can be implemented more widely.

Q4. What motivates you to do this work — what's your 'why'?

In my role, I help to create supply chains that are smarter, cleaner, and more resilient. Every improvement - whether reducing emissions, cutting waste, or improving efficiency - has a ripple effect that benefits businesses, communities, and the planet.
Because logistics touches almost every industry, collaboration is essential. When customers and suppliers work together, we can share both the costs and the benefits of meaningful change. What drives me is knowing that the work I do helps businesses operate more responsibly.

Q5. As a younger person working in a large, established industry, what has that experience been like for you?

Sustainability is still relatively new in the logistics sector, so I often get to be at the forefront of change. This does come with challenges, especially when introducing new ways of working to some team members who have been in the business longer than I have been alive! I've found that collaboration and communication are crucial to bring the team along with us, even if that takes time.

6. Finally, are there any books, podcasts, articles, or people that have shaped how you think about your work, leadership, or sustainability?

Akshat Rathi's book Climate Capitalism was a motivational read, which highlighted some of the key sustainability innovations that are being developed around the world. He discusses many heartening case studies that show that meaningful change is achievable, with or without government support. It's a reminder that innovation and collaboration are key to solving global challenges which I try to incorporate into my work every day.

Katelyn Prendiville – Head of Engagement at WorkforClimate and Co-Founder of SeedCulture

Katelyn is an Aussie who's spent most of her career exploring how people, culture and systems shape the big issues of our time - especially climate. Katelyn's background spans marketing, entrepreneurship, consulting, and now the NGO world, but the through-line has always been the same: helping people understand their own power to create change. She's fascinated by what motivates action, what gets in the way, and how workplaces can become real engines of climate progress rather than passive bystanders.

Q1. What first pulled you into this work? Was it one moment or a gradual realisation?

It was definitely a series of moments over many years. I spent nearly a decade in marketing, learning the power of storytelling, behavioural science, and how to engage people to take action. Then came an apparel startup (born partly from my Olympic equestrian ambitions!) where I sought to learn how to build an ethical, responsible business. The deeper I dug, the clearer it became: the decisions we make as citizens, employees, and business owners are key to changing the systems that are so destructive to people and planet.

That realisation shifted my career into sustainability. As a management consultant for organisations undergoing sustainability transformations, I saw firsthand the struggle they had to embed it across their business. I also noticed that there was a big untapped opportunity to bring their people on the journey with them.

So I founded SeedCulture, where we were helping organisations to embed sustainability into their culture. Our software tool was designed to upskill and engage their employees to hit their sustainability goals.

Today, I'm delighted to be part of WorkforClimate, a non-profit helping professionals to transform their organisations from the inside out. WfC offer online learning, tools, community, and mentorship for corporate employees, blending practical climate education with leadership and influence-building skills in a business context.

Q2. What part of your journey so far, experience, mindset, even mistakes, has helped you most in doing what you do now?

I think that a learning mindset is absolutely key for this work. Having a sense of curiosity, open mindedness, and willingness to listen to others is key for both staying sane, and effectively bringing others into the tent. This work can be complex and messy, and there's no single blueprint. A sense of humour helps too. Taking the work seriously is important; taking *yourself* too seriously is rarely helpful!

Q3. What are you working on right now that excites you, or what's coming next that you're proud of?

Right now, I'm really energised by being in the NGO world and getting to work on climate issues in a way that feels more honest and less constrained by corporate optimism. It's refreshing to look at the system with clearer eyes - without the beer goggles that can start to mask your sense of reality when working in the depths of corporate sustainability. I'm working on projects that explore internal influence and employee-led climate action, which is where I think some of the most promising momentum sits.

I'm also currently finishing my own book, which digs into how employees can reclaim power within corporate structures and organise themselves as a force for climate action. It challenges the idea that influence only flows from the top and looks at how workers (individually and collectively) can shift company priorities, reshape the culture, and push for decisions aligned with a liveable future.

Q4. Climate work can be gratifying but also exhausting. How do you stay motivated or grounded?

Probably a very common answer but getting out in nature, exercise, and staying connected with friends outside of the climate space, too! Anything that helps life feel fuller and more balanced, and that reminds me that joy and rest are part of the work.

Q5. For someone wanting to make a difference — whether they're 18 or 48 — what's one piece of advice you'd offer?

Just get started. Action begets action, and you'll learn so much along the way. And remember: your path doesn't need to look like anyone else's. Your skills, your background, your way of showing up... all of it is useful. You are genuinely needed.

Q6. Finally, are there any books, films, podcasts, or other resources that have shaped the way you think about energy, climate, or purpose?

It's a bit grim/terrifying, but definitely recommend Ministry for the Future by Kim Stanley Robinson – it's incredibly important for imagining what the coming decades might hold if we don't mobilise to solve this thing. Also Nate Hagen's 'Great Simplification' podcast. It can also be quite a lot to take in, but incredibly eye-opening and a reality check/reminder for anyone doing this work.

Laura Gemmell - Chief Executive, Eco Choice Aotearoa

Laura Gemmell is the Chief Executive of Eco Choice Aotearoa, New Zealand's official ecolabel. With a background in journalism and international development communications, Laura brings a strong focus on storytelling, transparency, and systems change to sustainability. She has worked across humanitarian, climate, and business contexts globally, and is passionate about building trust, empowering communities, and helping organisations take practical, credible steps toward a more sustainable future.

Q1. To start us off; who are you, what do you do, and what is Eco Choice Aotearoa?

Eco Choice Aotearoa is the Ministry for the Environment's official ecolabel. We've been around since 1992, and we certify products and services against really strict life-cycle criteria. We're aligned with ISO 14024, which is the international standard for Type I ecolabels.

What makes us a bit different from many other ecolabels globally is that we've chosen to include social accountability criteria alongside environmental performance. That's because sustainability isn't just about emissions or materials, it's also about people, health, and fairness. We take a really holistic view.

We're a not-for-profit, which honestly is a terrible business model in some ways. If a business meets our standards, they pay a licence fee to use the label. But if they don't meet the bar, they don't get through, even if that makes things harder for us financially. That independence is non-negotiable. If we start letting things slide, there's no reason for us to exist.

Q2. Your background isn't environmental science, how did you find your way into this work?

I actually started out as a journalist. I've always loved writing, and I've always had a strong sense of what feels just and unjust. Journalism felt like a way to inform people about issues that mattered and make complex things accessible.

I spent a big part of my career working in communications and public engagement for an international development and humanitarian aid agency. That took me all around the world. One thing I was really passionate about was helping communities tell their own stories — not being the well-meaning outsider parachuting in and speaking for them.

Over time, I started to see how much that work was being undermined by climate change. You could work alongside a community for decades — on education, health, livelihoods — and then a cyclone, drought, or sea-level rise would wipe so much of it out. I saw that very starkly in places like Indonesia and Afghanistan.

That domino effect of climate change really got under my skin. I wanted to understand the root causes better, so during COVID (with a four-month-old baby) I did some study around business sustainability. When the role at what was then Environmental Choice NZ came up, I looked at it and thought: the bones of this organisation are phenomenal. This is such a powerful lever for change, and hardly anyone seems to know it exists.

Q3. Why does this work matter so much to you personally?

I think it comes back to wanting people to be informed, but also wanting to give them something *tangible* they can do. Most people don't have the time or headspace to fact-check every product they buy or investigate supply chains. That's where a credible ecolabel can help.

I also really struggle with the idea that climate action is only for experts or activists. That mindset excludes people. We need more communicators, more creatives, more people from different backgrounds in this space. Frankly, the environmental movement has been pretty bad at storytelling and movement-building in the past, and we won't get the critical mass we need if we make perfection the entry fee.

Everyone has influence, whatever their role. People often underestimate that.

Q4. Eco Choice sits between consumers and businesses. How do you see your role in driving real change?

I loathe when the onus is put entirely on consumers. We've seen that with recycling — it's like, stop making plastic crap in the first place. Get to the core of the problem.

That said, we do straddle both sides. We work with businesses to continuously improve and reduce their impacts, and the ecolabel is the carrot; it gives them recognition and, hopefully, a market advantage. A lot of our impact is actually through procurement, influencing government and large organisations.

At the same time, individual actions *do* matter. Consumer choices can drive changes in packaging, ingredients, and supply chains. Voting matters too. So while I get frustrated with narratives that say individuals are powerless, I also don't believe responsibility should sit with them alone.

Our challenge is being nimble, communicating differently to different audiences, without losing credibility or focus. We try to be critical friends to business and government, and trusted guides for consumers.

Q5. Have mentors or role models shaped your leadership, and how do you approach leadership yourself?

I've been incredibly lucky. At Eco Choice, I've had a very supportive board who backed some pretty gutsy decisions — including a major rebrand and the introduction of social accountability criteria. They trusted us when the organisation was at a real crossroads.

Earlier in my life, my media studies teacher, Gordon Lawrence, was hugely influential, very high trust, very empowering. One of my first chief reporters at RNZ, Eileen Cameron, was intimidating in the best way and absolutely fought for her people. At World Vision, I worked with phenomenal female leaders who modelled leadership by clearing the path so others could do their best work.

I've never had formal leadership training, I feel like an accidental leader at times, but I've tried to model what I admired: trust, empathy, and removing obstacles for others. My job is to ask the team what's getting in their way and help remove it.

Q6. What advice would you give to young people who want to work in climate or sustainability?

Don't force yourself into a corner. You don't have to study sustainability or environmental science to make a difference, those skills are important, but they're not the only ones we need.

Start with what you're good at and what you enjoy. Are you a communicator? A finance nerd? A technologist? An artist? Then ask how *that* skill connects to climate and sustainability. That's how you carve out a niche without burning out.

Also, your job doesn't have to be everything. You can exert influence at work and still volunteer, sit on a board, or support causes outside your day job. Perfect jobs are rare, meaningful impact isn't.

And finally: you can't do everything. Figure out where you can make the most impact, focus there, and let others play their part too.

Mike Casey – CEO, Rewiring Aotearoa

Mike Casey is an entrepreneur and cherry orchardist from Central Otago who has electrified all the machines on his farm and demonstrated how transitioning away from diesel can save farmers tens of thousands of dollars each year and significantly reduce emissions. He is also the CEO of Rewiring Aotearoa, a New Zealand charity dedicated to electrifying millions of fossil fuel machines across the motu as quickly as possible.
"Whether in the home or on the farm, electrification is a real win-win. It's not just the right environmental decision anymore, it's the right economic decision. It's a no-brainer. We just have to figure out how to make it easy."

Q1. How did you go from software startup founder to electric-orchard farmer and climate advocate?

No plan, after selling my startup, we decided to buy a small farm south of Wanaka. We then decided to plant cherries because the yield on the land value was ok. Starting fresh and planting 9300 cherry trees, we needed to buy machines. I was a tech enthusiast and realised going electric was lower cost overall. Then once we went fully electric, I naturally started talking about it more and more, and being the loudmouth and attention seeker I am, became fairly effective at passing on the message that electricity was better than fossil fuels for so many reasons.

Q2. When did the idea of electrifying a farm first take hold?

I didn't, it simply started with one machine at a time, and then when we built our first solar system, we became really motivated to use energy we create ourselves. And then it just ballooned from there, with a bit of a realisation that we could create something special to add to the flavour.

Q3. Looking ahead, what does the future look like for you, and where do you see the most significant opportunities for young people and new jobs in the climate and electrification space?

Electrical Engineers, electricians and supporting trades. We have a big transition ahead of us. A nation-building opportunity. We have spent too long asking economists and accountants to solve climate, when in reality, we should have been asking practical people all along. The big opportunity is setting a national direction that's good for all of us.

4. Along your journey, were there mentors, role models, or people who shaped your thinking about climate solutions, agriculture, or electrification?

Yes, but not in the way you would think. I think I had a lot of people who believed in me and supported me to shift past the imposter syndrome and really refine my message. My wife is probably the single biggest support, and the funding we got for Rewiring Aotearoa from a number of key New Zealanders meant that I could move full-time into electrifying our nation, backed by a team of people far more brilliant than me!

5. If someone (whether 18 or 48) wanted to explore working in climate solutions, what advice would you give them?

Do something practical and focus on things that will actually shift the needle. Get stuck in and set a tangible example for others.

6. And finally, any books, films, podcasts or stories that have influenced your thinking or helped shape your philosophy on sustainability?

Saul Griffith had the biggest influence on me as an Author, a story of better lifestyles with electrification than the narrative of doom and gloom. I think focusing on what this could become if we do this right is far better than telling people to have shorter showers and walk extra miles. But my real influence comes from my team insider Rewiring, so I recommend checking out Investing in Tomorrow, that's a good narrative for NZ that's never been told before

Nick Loosley - Founder, Everybody Eats

Nick Loosley is the founder of Everybody Eats, a pay-what-you-can dining concept that turns surplus food into high-quality shared meals, bringing together people from all walks of life around the same table. What began as an experiment in hospitality has grown into an internationally recognised model tackling food waste, food insecurity, and social isolation, all at once.

Nick's work sits at the intersection of climate action and community wellbeing. By addressing food waste at scale while creating inclusive spaces, he demonstrates how everyday work — done differently — can reshape systems. He is a passionate advocate for using professional skills intentionally, and for recognising that the choices we make in our jobs often matter far more than the choices we make as consumers.

Q1. Everybody Eats is often described as a restaurant, a charity, and a community space all at once. In your own words, what is it, and what problem were you trying to solve when you started it?

Everybody Eats is a pay-what-you-can dining model built around surplus food that would otherwise go to waste. With a small team of staff and a huge volunteer base, we turn that food into three-course, restaurant-quality meals served at shared tables. The idea is simple but intentional: everyone gets the same food, service, and experience, whether they're food secure or not. It's about reducing food waste and food insecurity, but just as importantly, breaking down social isolation and hierarchy through something universal: good food shared together.

Q2. You didn't come to this work from outside hospitality; you redesigned it from within. How did your career in restaurants shape the solution you eventually built?

I'd spent years working in hospitality, including running higher-end restaurants, and I became increasingly frustrated with what I saw in the food system, waste, inequality, and a disconnect between value and access. I later studied at Schumacher College in the UK, where systems thinking and ecology helped me see food waste and food insecurity not as separate issues, but as part of the same broken system. My dissertation became the foundation for what would eventually become *Everybody Eats*. Rather than starting something in a sector I didn't understand, I chose to work within the industry I knew best. That meant I could focus less on learning the mechanics of hospitality and more on re-imagining its purpose. Everybody Eats exists because everything aligned: experience, passion, and a willingness to question the default way things are done.

Q3. Volunteers play a huge role in Everybody Eats. Why do you think people choose to show up, and what does that say about culture at work more broadly?
People volunteer because the mission is clear and authentic: reduce waste, reduce food insecurity, and reduce social isolation. Different volunteers connect with different parts of

that, but very few disagree with any of it. What's interesting is that once you get the intention right, culture largely takes care of itself. Our volunteers have chosen to be there — and that choice shows up as generosity, warmth, and care. In many workplaces, organisations try to "build culture" after the fact. We've seen that when values are genuinely embedded, people reinforce them for you.

Q4. You've spoken about how people often overestimate the impact of individual consumption and underestimate the impact of their work. How did that insight shape your own decisions?

We're constantly told that the biggest climate or social impact we can have is through what we buy. But in reality, the biggest influence most of us have is as producers, as employees, creators, managers, and leaders. Once I recognised that, I made a conscious decision to spend my working life trying to solve problems rather than unintentionally adding to them. That's a privileged choice, and not everyone can do it in the same way, but the principle still holds: your job shapes systems far more than your shopping basket ever will.

Q5. This kind of work can be intense. How do you think about balance, leadership, and staying grounded over the long term?

I've learned that balance isn't about rigid rules, it's about self-awareness. I've engineered my work around how I function best, not how society says I should. Sometimes that means exercising at 10am on a Wednesday; sometimes it means taking a call on a Sunday evening. I'm intentional about where my energy goes, and I regularly reflect on whether work, family, health, and friendships are all getting enough attention. Leadership, for me, has shifted from being reactive to being more coaching-oriented, both with others and with myself.

Q6. For someone reading this who wants to make a positive impact through their work, but feels constrained by money, time, or responsibility, what advice would you offer?

Take time to understand the problem before trying to solve it. We're very good at creating solutions that accidentally generate new issues. If you can, get really good at something first, depth matters. Change doesn't have to be dramatic or immediate; it can be incremental, alongside paid work, through volunteering or side projects. Not everyone can take a year out or start a charity, but everyone has some agency. The key is recognising that your work already has impact; the question is whether it's intentional.

Stuart Goldsmith - Climate Comedian

Stuart Goldsmith is an internationally award-winning climate comedian and speaker who uses stand-up comedy to engage audiences with the climate crisis.

His television credits include *Live at the Apollo, and* Conan O'Brien. His work has been featured across major media outlets including BBC Radio, BBC News, Radio Times, and News UK. Stuart's 2023 solo show *Spoilers* won Best Show at the Leicester Comedy Festival and was one of the most acclaimed shows at the Edinburgh Fringe Festival, where it played to sell-out audiences.

His stand-up special *I Need You Alive* is available online, and he is currently developing his second climate comedy hour. Stuart performs internationally at festivals, conferences, and corporate events, using comedy to spark engagement, reflection, and relief from climate dread. He is also the host of the globally recognised *Comedian's Comedian* podcast, which has surpassed 25 million downloads.

Q1. For those who might not know you, who are you, what do you do, and how did you end up becoming a "climate comedian"?

My name is Stuart Goldsmith, and I'm a climate comedian — a term I didn't invent, but one I've leaned into because there aren't many of us. I'm a professional stand-up comedian who has chosen to focus my work on the climate crisis and everything that unravels once you start pulling that thread:

258

inequality, power, economics, responsibility, the Sustainable Development Goals — all of it.

Comedy has always been how I work out what I think. I don't sit down with a manifesto. I do material about what's on my mind, and then a year later I realise, "Oh, wow, I guess I was really going through something."

That "something" was climate dread.

In 2022, I was doing a work-in-progress show at the Edinburgh Festival. At the start of the month, I had about five minutes on climate — specifically all the tricks I use to convince myself that everything's going to be fine. By the end of the month, I had about twenty-five minutes on it, and I wanted more.

What I learned is that grappling with the climate can actually be engaging. Even enjoyable, in moments. It's less scary than avoiding it, and it helps with climate dread. That became the heart of my work.

I don't work in sustainability in the formal sense, but my job is a climate job. I talk about climate because it's the thing I find most compelling, difficult, and creatively fulfilling. And as an artist, that's what keeps me interested.

Q2. You've been a comedian for a long time. What changed around 2021–22 that pulled climate to the centre of your work?

I've been a comedian for about twenty years. I've never had a "real job" in the traditional sense. I was a street performer in Covent Garden before I was a stand-up — that's my CV.

Around the pandemic, a few things collided. I'd done a huge amount of comedy, and novelty had always been a big part of what sustained me. Then suddenly, everything stopped. I was at home with two small children, which I loved, but I was also deeply worried about the climate.

I'd watched COVID creep from page thirty of the news to the front page, and I'd been watching climate do the same thing for years. That was unsettling.

At the same time, I'd started doing more work with businesses through my podcast *The Comedian's Comedian* and keynote talks about resilience. I realised I liked talking to people who were trying to do good work inside organisations.

When I started talking about climate on stage, two things happened: it helped me process my own anxiety, and it gave my comedy a renewed sense of purpose. Suddenly, I wasn't bored anymore. I was learning, researching, and desperately wanting to say things.

That's when it clicked.

Q3. You've spoken about discovering that your "job is a climate job". How did that realisation land for you?

There's a brilliant climate thinker in the US, Dr Ayana Elizabeth Johnson, who talks about a climate Venn diagram: something the climate needs, something you love doing, and something you're good at.

That idea lodged itself in my brain.

I realised that comedy is the thing I'm good at, the thing I love, and something the climate needs — not facts alone, but communication, engagement, and relief from despair.

Comedy doesn't change the world. Comedy changes people, and people change the world.

My concrete circumstances as a comedian matter here. I look and sound like a "nice guy". When I walk on stage, people relax. I've got decades of experience being in front of people. That presence can actually hold me back in traditional comedy — audiences often want awkward weirdos — but in climate communication, it's a superpower.

I can stand in front of powerful people in nice suits and make them listen. I can put sticky, memorable jokes into their heads that resurface later when they're making decisions.

That's my instrument in the orchestra.

Q4. Your work seems very intentional, even if you don't describe it as a strategy. How do you think about impact?

I wouldn't call it a strategy document, but stand-up itself is built on iteration. You try things, you fail, you learn fast. Sometimes nightly.

One thing I've learned as a comedian is that if I think something is funny, it *is* funny. If it doesn't land, that's a communication failure, not an idea failure. That gives you resilience.

The same applies here. I don't have to solve the climate crisis. I don't need all the answers. I just need to be honest, informed, flexible, and willing to grapple.

That word — grapple — is everything. Climate work is one long grapple. It won't be "solved" in our lifetimes, and weirdly, I find that comforting. I just want to do the best I can, for as long as I can, using the tools I have.

Sometimes that's awareness. Sometimes it's relief. Sometimes it's putting the right thought in front of the right person at the right moment.

Q5. You spend a lot of time with sustainability professionals and organisations. What have you learned from working in that space?

I love working with what I call "corporate work for the good guys". The vibe is different. People genuinely care.

That said, it's complex. Someone once told me that the amount of money you make is often inversely proportional to how much good you're doing. That stings.

Another person pointed out that sustainability teams don't exist to save the world — they exist to manage organisational risk. That also stings. But both can be true.

I've met so many people trying to do good work from inside imperfect systems. People who could go and work for a "perfect" organisation, but choose not to because they want to change something harder.

That's real work.

I also wrestle openly with contradictions: flying, consumption, individual action versus systemic change. I don't want to make audiences feel powerless, but I also don't want to pretend individual action alone will save us.

That tension is the material.

Q6. If a young person told you they want to "work in climate" but don't know what that means yet, what would you say?

First: great. That's a good instinct.

Second: no one knows what the world of work will look like in ten years, especially with AI. So don't over-plan.

My real advice would be: talk to people. Ask for meetings. If you're seventeen, people will say yes. Buy them a coffee. Ask questions.

One thing I've learned from comedy is that people who ask for help tend to progress faster. There's often a gender divide there — men think they have to solve everything alone; women build networks more effectively. Be the second one.

Get obsessed with something. Pick a thing and go deep. It's much easier to move sideways once you're good at something than to move forward when you've dabbled in ten things.

And build human skills. Robots can't shake hands or look people in the eye. Community, communication, and empathy will matter more, not less.

Q7. Is there anything you'd want to leave readers with?

You are not required to play a solo.

That idea changed my life. We're all part of the same orchestra. Find the instrument in your hands and play it as well as you can. That's enough.

Tara Spencer - Sustainability Advisor at Reclaim Ltd

Tara is a Sustainability Advisor, "aka professional trash talker" (her words), at Reclaim (recycling & waste management), working with clients to improve their recycling and reduce waste to landfill. She runs in-person and virtual education sessions for organisations across Aotearoa New Zealand, doing waste audits, and running the Recycle.co.nz social media accounts, and much more - anything to help people reduce waste and see recyclable material as a valuable resource.

Tara also assists with running Recycling Week, Aotearoa New Zealand's largest annual campaign on waste and recycling education. Recycling Week is a free campaign, designed to make learning about waste minimisation easy and fun. Go to https://rwhub.reclaim.co.nz/ to register - They'd love to have you/ your organisation join in!

Q1. Could you tell us a bit about your career journey so far, and how you came to be working in recycling and resource recovery today?

I was never one of those kids that knew exactly what they wanted to be when they grow up. All I knew for sure was that I wanted to end up in a career that helped people, and I wanted to help make the world a better place. My dad spent his entire career working for a forestry company, so the concept of sustainability (in the more literal sense) was something I was raised with.

After I finished my undergraduate degree in psychology I wasn't sure what to do next. I wasn't ready for the additional years of postgrad tertiary study necessary for careers in my degree, and I still wasn't sure what I wanted to actually do with my life. I started out in the legal sector, sort of by accident - initially various administration work, which turned into Legal Secretary work while studying to be a registered Legal Executive. At the time, law felt like a stable, sensible, "safe" career. The people were great, but the high-stakes nature of the work, the long hours, and under-resourcing meant that I was constantly highly stressed. In an effort to stay sane and retain some enjoyment in the role, I started up a Sustainability Committee at the firm. I could see that there were many things that we could do to lighten our footprint, and so I wrangled a surprisingly large and enthusiastic team of lawyers and support staff into various small initiatives - introducing a compost bin in the lunchroom, making sure lights were turned off in empty offices, removing desk bins, trialling snacks in reusable packaging and vegetarian morning teas (although that one almost caused a riot - it turns out that people can become borderline violent when their access to sausage rolls is revoked!). Even then, I was the crazy person who would sort out the waste people had mistakenly put in the recycling bins, and became the go-to person for my colleagues' sustainability and waste questions.

After five years working in law I was completely burnt out, and ready to for a change to a more purpose-driven role. I was fortunate enough to have the means and support to take a gap year of sorts to do some further study, with the aim of transitioning to a career in something that I'd always felt drawn to and had done of my own volition in my previous role: sustainability. The news reports about the state of the environment seemed to be increasingly dire, and I desperately wanted to end up in a role where I could contribute positively.

During my studies, I would trawl Seek, LinkedIn and other similar sites, looking at the descriptions for entry-level sustainability roles. Many of them had some mention of waste and waste audits, so when I saw an ad for a Waste Auditor role on Student Job Search, I jumped on the chance and applied. The Sustainability Manager of Reclaim called me, and we instantly clicked. The waste auditor role was purely labour, but she mentioned that there was also a potential opening at the company to assist with Recycling Week. I was brought on part time to assist with preparation for that year's Recycling Week campaign, and shortly afterwards, I was brought onto the team full time as a Sustainability Advisor. This is the role I have held for just over three years now.

While it's certainly not the most glamorous of roles, knowing that our efforts are helping to avoid waste and keep precious natural resources out of landfill is genuinely thrilling. Having meaningful conversations about waste and recycling and seeing people have lightbulb moments when they learn something and commit to making changes is such a buzz and I am so glad to have taken the leap and transitioned to a new career.

Q2. What motivated you to make the shift into this space, and what were some of the challenges or uncertainties you had to navigate along the way?

The desire to reduce my climate anxiety and make a positive difference to a wider circle than just my friends and family was my main motivator for shifting into the resource recovery space. The seemingly endless bombardment of headlines that we've breached another planetary boundary, that there's been yet another "once in a lifetime" natural disaster, that we're soon going to have more plastic than fish in the ocean, that another native species is on the verge of extinction... it can leave us feeling paralysed, hopeless, like nothing we do can hold back the tide. I found that the best way to deal with the anxiety was to take action, even if it was just in small, personal ways. Making changes, seeing how they added up, and talking to people about these actions made the anxiety feel less severe. But eventually, small personal actions weren't enough to assuage the climate anxiety and I felt the need to widen the net. Starting the Sustainability Committee in my role at the time helped make me feel better about the impact of my work, and from there I knew I needed to have sustainability be a part of my career.

My initial challenge was not lack of support, but lack of confidence. I was fortunate to have support from the firm in establishing the Sustainability Committee, and staff ranging from secretaries to junior lawyers to Partners put their hands up to participate, but I didn't trust myself to lead as strongly. Some people are inherently confident and outspoken (or at least do a great job of appearing that way!), whereas I take some time to build that confidence. Once in a full-time sustainability role, something I initially struggled with was imposter syndrome, feeling as though I wasn't qualified or knowledgeable enough to be there. The waste and recycling space in Aotearoa is small, with most people spending the majority of their careers bouncing between a small group of companies, so many of my colleagues have decades of knowledge and experience that I did not have. There was (and still is!) a lot to learn in a constantly evolving space, and this initially felt overwhelming. Fortunately, my colleagues at Reclaim have always made time for my questions and have generously shared their seemingly endless knowledge, and I was able to quickly get up to speed.

Q3. What does your day-to-day work in recycling actually look like, and what might surprise people about how this part of the system really operates?

While recycling is very much normalised here in Aotearoa (according to the latest research from MfE, around 97% of Kiwis recycle), there is still a lot of confusion about how to do it right. My role at Reclaim therefore largely comes down to education and behaviour change - communicating best-practice waste minimisation and recycling to groups of people from all backgrounds and levels of knowledge and experience with the goal of reducing contamination in recycling, and reducing the amount of waste generated in the first place. The day-to-day role is quite varied. The bulk of the work involves either digging through waste (leading waste audits for clients), talking about waste (running education sessions for corporate groups on recycling and waste minimisation, and responding to recycling queries from the public), or thinking about waste (preparing educational videos and social media posts, leading internal initiatives, and more). Another huge part of my role is helping to coordinate New Zealand's annual Recycling Week - a free educational campaign designed to make waste minimisation easy and fun. I truly love my job. I cannot go anywhere now without having a nosy at the bins - when travelling, my camera roll inevitably ends up with a bunch of pictures of different bins and their signage!

Waste and recycling tends to be something you don't really think about until you are forced to. Most people put stuff in a recycling bin and assume that someone, somewhere, will turn it into something new. The stuff disappears when the bin gets emptied, and that's where conscious thought tends to end - out of sight, out of mind. Many people may be surprised to realise that just because something is put in a recycling bin, it doesn't necessarily mean that it will actually get recycled. Whether something gets recycled largely depends on whether it is put in the right bin, the type of material it's made from, whether it is contaminated, and whether there is an end market for the material. The sheer volume of stuff received through residential kerbside recycling means that only the main types and grades of material (paper and cardboard, glass bottles and jars, aluminium and metal cans, and select plastic grades, depending on the Council) get separated out for recycling. Just because you put a broken jandal in your home recycling bin and hope for the best, doesn't mean it can or will be recycled! You might even be contaminating other actually recyclable material.

Q4. From your perspective, where do individuals and businesses have the biggest opportunity to improve our environmental and/or social impact?

Every person has a sphere of influence, both individually and through our communities and our jobs. Some people's spheres are larger than others, and our spheres are limited by the time, resources, abilities, access and privilege we have, but nevertheless we all have our spheres. One of the biggest opportunities we have to improve our environmental and social impact is to use our power as consumers (both on an individual and commercial level) to make conscious and environmentally responsible decisions. It is very important to make sure we put things in the right waste or recycling bins, but ultimately this is like mopping up water that is overflowing from a bathtub. Instead of relying on endlessly mopping up water, the better thing to do is turn off the tap. Producers only make the things we buy! By avoiding buying unnecessary things, making more sustainable and ethical purchasing decisions, reducing the amount of stuff we purchase, and reusing, sharing, repairing and repurposing what we already have, we can all gradually turn off our taps. This has much greater upstream effects than just on the amount of stuff in our bins each week - by being more conscious of what we consume as individuals and what we produce in our workplaces, we can reduce the need to extract precious non-renewable resources from the earth, prevent single-use things from being made, reduce energy use, stop supporting billionaires and instead support local businesses that pay their workers a living wage, and make sure vital ancient skills are maintained.

Q5. For someone reading this who's considering a career change or wondering how to move into more purpose-driven work, what advice would you offer?

My advice to anyone considering a career change or looking to move into more purpose-driven work would be to see if there are opportunities to introduce elements of this into your existing job. If there are no opportunities already there in your organisation, try creating your own. As corny as it sounds, be the change you wish to see in the world! Join your organisation's Green Team, or if there isn't one, see if you can start one. You may be surprised at how many other people there are who also want to act, but just need someone to step up and lead. This will not only improve the operations of your existing organisation, but also give you valuable experience that you can leverage to move in the direction you want to head in your future career. Join local community groups that are doing the kind of thing you're passionate about - you will meet similarly-minded people and this might lead to further opportunities down the line.

Qiulae Wong - Leader of The Opportunity Party

Qiulae 'Q' Wong is the Leader of the Opportunity Party in Aotearoa New Zealand. She has spent her career championing ethical business, sustainability, and purpose-driven change — first in roles spanning human rights, ethical fashion and impact consulting in London, and later leading the B Corp movement in New Zealand and advising major corporations on low-carbon transition at KPMG.

Born and raised in Auckland, Q studied law and politics before moving overseas, where she co-founded a sustainability tech start-up and led teams focused on flexible, purpose-led work. Since returning home, she has also served as co-convenor of Kiwis in Climate and as a Trustee of the Wellbeing Economy Alliance Aotearoa.

In her current role, she brings her experience in business, policy and climate advocacy into politics, with a focus on building resilient, connected communities and harnessing business as a force for positive change.

Q1. To start us off, what do you currently do, and what led you to your most recent career shift?

I'm the Leader of The Opportunity Party (TOP), a relatively small political party in Aotearoa New Zealand that hasn't yet made it into Parliament. And honestly, I never set out to become a politician.

I studied politics and law at university, but when MPs came to speak in lectures, the job looked incredibly stressful — and it didn't seem like the most effective way to make change. So I went into the private sector, where I spent around 15 years, including nine in London, working mostly in the fashion industry and later in broader sustainability consulting.

What I realised over time is that even when you work with brilliant, values-aligned companies — the "1–2%" trying to operate differently — you're still only changing the margins. If you want new norms, new rules, and a new direction for society, government and politics are where that ultimately happens.

TOP is the only political home where I've felt I don't have to compromise on my values. It's about doing things differently, from democratic processes to economic incentives, and bringing bold, fresh ideas forward. My work in the B Corp and purpose-led business world has given me a lot to bring into politics.

Q2. For context, can you explain B Corp and why it shaped your approach?

B Corp is, in my view, the best business certification in the world. It's about helping businesses balance purpose with profit. The movement challenges what one of the founders famously called the "source code error of capitalism", the idea that companies must maximise short-term profit above all else.

Instead, B Corp requires companies to consider all stakeholders: nature, employees, customers, suppliers, and communities. It reframes business as something that should contribute positively to society, not extract from it. Historically, businesses were created to solve social problems, transporting goods, building infrastructure, and feeding populations, but we lost sight of that. B Corp helps bring us back.

Q3. For readers not from New Zealand. How would you describe the current political landscape here, and where TOP fits?

New Zealand uses an MMP (Mixed Member Proportional) system, which is meant to ensure more diverse representation. And while it has worked in many ways, recent years have mirrored global trends: increasing polarisation, identity politics, and major parties drifting to opposite extremes.

Despite MMP, we've ended up with something that behaves like a two-bloc system — left vs right — rather than collaborative governance. This polarisation makes it hard to agree on long-term issues like infrastructure, economic direction, or climate action.

TOP positions itself as *radical centrist*. We believe many New Zealanders sit in the middle — wanting pragmatic, evidence-based solutions but unsure who truly represents them. Our goal is to build common ground and move the country forward rather than deepen division.

Q4. For someone considering politics as a pathway for impact, how should they choose a party or place to work?

Someone once told me that *politics is the art of the possible*. You might hold a vision for the world you want to help create, but no one hands you a magic wand. If you're lucky, you might pass a few pieces of meaningful legislation in your career.

So the first question is:
What are the one or two big changes I most want to help make?

For me, those are:

1. An economy that doesn't extract more from people and nature than it gives back
2. Stronger community connection and understanding between people

Once you know your purpose, you can identify the political vehicle most aligned with delivering it. That applies beyond politics, too — every job becomes more meaningful when you anchor yourself to your personal "why".

Q5. The word "sustainability" shows up everywhere now. What do you tell young people who say they "want to work in sustainability"?

"Sustainability" has definitely lost some meaning — it means wildly different things to different people.

A better starting point is:
What part of sustainability matters most to you?

Is it biodiversity? Fair wages? Supply chains? Emissions? Circular design? Community wellbeing?

Once you find the part that sparks you, match it with your skills. Sustainability needs:

- financial modelling
- storytelling and communication
- policy and systems thinking
- legal expertise
- data and analytics
- design and product development
- community and cultural leadership

In my own career, I've done comms, data work, facilitation, consulting, and experience reveals where you're happiest and most effective.

Q6. What originally sparked your own journey into ethical and sustainable work?

I've always had a strong sense of social justice, even if I couldn't articulate it early on. My first role after university was working for my sister, who ran a social change communications agency. We worked on a disability-inclusion campaign funded by the Ministry of Social Development, helping businesses understand the financial and social value of accessibility.

That was my first eye-opening experience of *business as a force for good*.

I've also always loved fashion; I studied design at school purely out of creative joy. When I moved to London, I wanted to combine that creativity with purpose. Through roles at the Ethical Fashion Forum and others, I learned about ethical sourcing, supply chains, labour issues, and environmental impacts. It was never a grand plan, just following the things I cared about.

Q7. Have mentors played a role in your journey?

Absolutely. Pretty much everyone I've worked for has been a mentor in some form.

My sister was a major early influence. And I've learned, looking back, that when you're young you often *don't realise* you're being mentored. You're impatient, convinced you know everything, and frustrated things aren't moving fast enough!

The mentors who've had the biggest impact all shared one thing:
They asked great questions.
They didn't give me the answers — they helped me find them.

That's what I try to do now when I'm in the mentoring role.

Q8. Politics is demanding. How do you manage burnout and stay grounded?

My two daughters keep me busy, which is wonderful but leaves little downtime. When I do get a spare half-hour, exercise is my anchor. Running is my meditation; it helps me synthesise thoughts and decompress quickly. I also love yoga, though I struggle to find the longer stretches of time it requires.

Otherwise, it's family and friends. I'm lucky to have a tight-knit group locally and a close group of school friends. People, community, exercise, those are the basics that keep me grounded.

Q9. Any books, podcasts, or resources that have shifted your perspective recently?

I'm re-reading *Reinventing Organisations* by Frederic Laloux, which explores "teal organisations" — decentralised, trust-based, less hierarchical ways of working. I read it in a business context years ago; now I'm exploring its relevance to politics.

The Great Simplification Podcast is another big one. It's dense, but once you digest the ideas, it genuinely shifts your worldview.

Is there anything you'd like to leave readers with?

Everything — climate, nature, politics, communities — comes back to how well we understand each other as people. If we can listen more openly, build more connection, and humanise one another beyond the online world, then I think everything else becomes possible.

Human connection is the foundation for all the change we want to make.

From Inspiration to Action

You've just heard from people shaping climate action through policy, engineering, education, finance, logistics, recruitment, farming, construction, technology, comedy, community organising, and leadership. Some are CEOs. Some are teachers. Some are analysts, recruiters, founders, engineers, communicators, and quietly influential people working deep inside complex systems.

None of them started fully ready.
Most didn't start in sustainability at all.

They began where they were, with the skills they had, and worked things out as they went.

Before moving on, it's worth pausing to zoom out and notice what sits beneath all of these conversations.

There is no single pathway here.
Entertainment. Recruitment. Policy. Software. Customer service. HVAC. Education. Hospitality. Journalism. Marketing. Engineering. Politics. Cherries. Finance. Logistics.

The list is deliberately messy because real careers are messy.

No one followed a straight line. They built one.

Across every interview, a few patterns kept surfacing.

First, almost everyone described asking questions. Why is this done this way? Why hasn't this changed? Why does this system create the outcome it does? Curiosity showed up in customer service roles, on building sites, inside banks, in classrooms, and in boardrooms. It was often the thing that opened the next door.

Second, saying yes. They often said yes before they felt ready. They put their hand up. They took on responsibility early. They tried things that weren't in the job description. Confidence rarely came first. Action did.

Third, people. Mentors. Colleagues. Communities. Networks. Coffee chats. Volunteering. Industry groups. Boards. Peer learning. None of these journeys happened in isolation. Progress came from connection, not individual brilliance.

And finally, again and again, people described moving from thinking "what can I do as a consumer" to "what can I influence through my work". Not "what can I buy?", but "what can I do, build or design?"

That shift matters. Because your job shapes systems. Buildings. Energy. Food. Transport. Finance. Education. Procurement. Culture. Policy. Technology. Your work is where leverage lives.

From CEOs and organisational leaders like Laura, Qiulae, Andrew, Emily and Mike, we see how leadership is less about having all the answers and more about setting direction, removing barriers, and backing people to do better. Whether it's defining what "good" looks like in buildings, making electrification the obvious economic choice, or protecting credibility in ecolabelling, leadership shows up as clarity, communication, and long-term thinking.

From recruitment and people-focused roles, like Amy's work at Hays, we see how values are now shaping the job market itself.

Sustainability is no longer a nice-to-have. Candidates are actively seeking purpose-aligned work, and employers are realising that values, culture, and climate literacy are essential for attracting and retaining talent. If you work in hiring, HR, leadership, or people strategy, you are quietly shaping the future workforce.

From educators like Charlotte, we're reminded that climate action is not abstract. It's taught, practiced, and built. Education that connects theory to hands-on experience creates confidence, competence, and dignity. Teaching people how to build well, communicate clearly, and solve real problems might be one of the most powerful climate interventions we have.

From people working deep inside finance and logistics, like Andy and Jodi, we see that not all climate work is visible. Pricing models, capital allocation, emissions data, and freight systems quietly shape the real economy. Decisions made far from headlines often determine what scales and what doesn't.

From communicators and storytellers like Stuart, Anje, and many of the others, we see the power of language. Stuart uses humour to lower defences and help people sit with uncomfortable truths. Anje translates dense, technical concepts into stories people can actually engage with. Graham Hendra does the same with engineering, using plain language and humour to make complex technology usable. Different stages, same lesson. If people don't understand something, it doesn't matter how good it is.

From founders and community builders like Nick, Emily, Katelyn, and Esther, we're reminded that you don't need permission to start. Community building, education, and behaviour change are not soft skills. They are foundational. Confidence often comes after action, not before. Impact scales when you enable others, grow volunteer bases, build networks, and create spaces where people feel invited rather than judged.

For many of the experiences we've just read, we see how purpose-driven work often grows from small, self-started initiatives rather than grand career plans. For Tara, she didn't begin in "sustainability" on paper; she began by noticing what didn't sit right, starting a committee, asking questions, and taking action where she already was. Her journey highlights the power of education, behaviour change, and confidence built through doing, and reminds us that tackling climate anxiety often starts with widening your sphere of influence, one practical step at a time.

Across all of these stories, kindness stands out. Generosity with time. Willingness to explain. Patience with learners. A belief that people, when supported properly, will step up.

If something you read sparked a thought, a challenge, or a flicker of possibility, follow it. Reach out. Learn more. Try something.

I want to say this clearly. I am deeply grateful to everyone who shared their time, insight, and honesty for this book. Each person gave more than they had to. This section exists because of that generosity.

What comes next is the Further Resources section, a practical companion to the people you've just met. You'll find tools, learning platforms, job links, books, podcasts, and people worth following.

You don't need to do all of it. Please don't try.

Just choose one entry point.
Start small.
Keep going.

That's how this work actually happens.

Conclusion — Your Job is a Climate Job

If you've made it this far, thank you. It means you care. And congratulations on persevering with this book, or you've become an elite speed-reader who skipped half the pages and jumped straight to the ending, hoping to see if we've magically solved the climate crisis.

Sadly, not.

But I'm glad you've stuck around.

This book started with a simple frustration: that we're often told climate change is everyone's responsibility, while being given very little clarity about where our *actual* influence sits. We're encouraged to optimise our personal lives down to the last yoghurt pot, while the systems that shape emissions, inequality, and environmental damage largely remain unchanged.

Along the way, we've unpacked some uncomfortable truths.
That responsibility is unevenly distributed.
That power and emissions are concentrated.
That many of the biggest levers for change don't sit in our kitchens or shopping baskets, but in workplaces, supply chains, policies, budgets, designs, and decisions.

You've read about the crisis.
But you've also read about the opportunity.

You've explored how your skills, your role, and your workplace already shape outcomes — whether you realised it or not.
You've seen how leaders, parents, engineers, consultants,

teachers, designers, activists, and quietly influential people are already doing this work in very different ways.

Their paths are all different, but they share one thing in common:

They started.

Not when they were "qualified enough".
Not when the perfect job appeared.
Not when the world was ready.

They began where they stood, with what they had, and let action build direction.

That's the real invitation of this book.

Not to have everything figured out.
Not to become someone else.
But to begin.

To let your values meet your work.
To notice where you already have influence.
To ask better questions.
To find others walking the same way.
To stay curious. Stay human. Stay optimistic — not blindly, but bravely.

My hope is that you close this book feeling slightly less powerless the next time you're standing at home sorting the recycling — and a little more purposeful when you walk into work tomorrow.

That you start looking at your job differently.
At meetings differently.
At projects, budgets, designs, and decisions differently.

That you realise influence already exists in your hands — not just in grand gestures, but in small, ordinary moments: what gets prioritised, what gets questioned, what gets normalised, and what quietly gets changed.

Final Thoughts

- Every job can be a climate job.
- Every system was built — and can be rebuilt.
- Every action matters. Every conversation matters. Every person matters.

You don't need to lead a movement, write policy, or launch a startup tomorrow (though if you do, genuinely — amazing). You just need to take one step.

Start a conversation.
Ask a question.
Join a project.
Encourage someone else.
Share what you know.
Read the next book.
Keep going.

This work is hard.
At times, it's slow.
Some days it will feel like shouting into the wind.

But you are not doing it alone.
And you are not doing it for nothing.

The people whose stories you've read in these pages — and the thousands more working quietly all over the world — are proof that change is already happening. In boardrooms and classrooms. In communities and workshops. In spreadsheets and site huts. In living rooms, labs, studios, and staff rooms.

And now, hopefully, wherever you are too.

When it gets heavy, take a breath.
Go for a walk.
Call someone.
Touch grass.
Go for a swim.
Watch the tide move in and out and remember that we're part of something much bigger — and something still very much in motion.

And tomorrow, try again.

Close the book.
Open a new chapter.

No perfect answers.
Just the willingness to act.

The future needs engineers and artists.
Storytellers and scientists.
Parents and policymakers.
Leaders, learners —
and people like you.

Your job is a climate job.
Whether you've known it all along,
or only just realised it now.

Welcome to the work.

Author's Note

I wrote this book because I wanted to do something. Something useful. Something tangible. Something that might help, even in a small way.

This book took a couple of years to write, but in truth it's the product of much more than that. It's grown out of years of conversations, projects, travel, meetings, half-formed ideas, late nights, and hours (feels like days) sat in traffic thinking; *there has to be a better way to do this*. It's been shaped by people I've met across different countries, industries, and communities, and by seeing first-hand both how much we have, and how much there is to lose.

Along the way, I've been lucky enough to work alongside people who share a few things in common. They care deeply. They're passionate. Their work rarely fits neatly into office hours. And many seem to carry a quiet, restless sense of wanting to do more, even when they're already doing so much.

These are people who want more out of life than a job title or a payslip. People who care about trees and tech, oceans and spreadsheets, biodiversity and boardrooms. People who understand that changing a system usually doesn't start with a master plan, but with a conversation, a connection, or an awkward first step that feels slightly uncomfortable at the time.

I don't pretend to have all the answers. I'm still learning, and I always will be.

This book isn't a destination or a manifesto. It's a snapshot, shaped by the people I've met, the places I've been, the mistakes I've made, and the questions I'm still trying to work through. There's a strange tension in this work: a constant sense that you could always be doing more, while also needing to recognise the value of what *is* being done.

Writing this book has deepened my appreciation for what we have, for the systems and environments we rely on every day, and for how unevenly both the benefits and burdens are shared around the world. It's reinforced for me that climate work isn't abstract. It's personal. It's social. It's economic. It's about work, yes, but also animals, homes, health, culture, nature, politics, dignity, and opportunity.

It's also reminded me how much of this work is held together by relationships. Coffees squeezed between meetings. Beers after long days. Messages sent across time zones. Conversations full of hope one week and frustration the next, especially when policy shifts, markets wobble, or progress feels slower than it should.

If reading this has given you something, even if it's as small as the confidence to ask your boss what happens to the office waste, then I'm happy with that. And if it made you think, question, or see your own work or career path a little differently, then that's great too.

All around the world, there are so many people doing incredible work, and documenting or sharing their own experiences, research and work. In the pages that follow, I've shared some of the books, voices, and ideas that continue to shape my own thinking.

Further Resources

Education, job opportunities, books, podcasts, creators, and tools to deepen your understanding, stay informed, and connect with the global climate community.

Use these as a starting point, not a definitive list. Follow curiosity. Pursue what resonates. Let one resource lead you to the next. The most important thing is to keep learning, keep listening, and keep moving.

Education is a Climate Solution

Learning isn't just preparation for climate action, it *is* climate action. The more people understand how systems work, where emissions come from, and what solutions already exist, the faster we can shift behaviours, industries and policies.

Education helps us build informed advocacy, challenge outdated assumptions, empower communities, inspire innovation, and create the skilled workforce we need for a just transition.

You don't need to study environmental science to contribute. Whether you're on a construction site, in a classroom, at a board table or behind a bar, learning more about climate and sustainability gives you the language, awareness and confidence to influence decisions in whatever space you occupy.

Curiosity is a climate tool. Knowledge is leverage. And the more of us that understand what needs to change, the harder it becomes for things to stay the same.

And the best part? Much of this learning is *free and accessible to anyone with an internet connection.*

Here are some great places to begin your learning journey, at *zero cost*:

RESOURCE	WHAT IT OFFERS
UN SDG LEARN	Short online courses across sustainability, policy, climate diplomacy and more.
MIT OPENCOURSEWARE – ENVIRONMENT COLLECTION	Free university-level courses covering energy, climate science and sustainable technology.
SDG ACADEMY	Online courses from global climate and sustainability experts.
OPEN UNIVERSITY (UK)	Free courses including sustainability, environmental science and systems thinking.
LINKEDIN LEARNING	Free modules (sometimes fully unlocked via schools/businesses) on ESG, sustainability strategy, climate leadership.
CLIMATE FRESK	Interactive workshops helping people understand climate science through collaboration.

WORKFORCLIMATE	Courses and tools to help people accelerate climate action inside their organisations.

If you're not ready for a full course, start with a podcast, read one article a week, or watch a single short video. Little steps count.

There is no set path into climate work, only a willingness to learn. Whether through formal study, apprenticeships, lived experience or self-directed learning, what matters is momentum, not perfection.

if children don't grow up learning about and appreciating nature, they won't understand its importance, won't protect it, and then "who will?"

Jobs & Signposting

If you're exploring roles in sustainability or climate-focused careers and aren't sure where to look, LinkedIn can be an invaluable place to start. Many professionals actively share job opportunities, industry insights and hiring trends. Finding the right people to follow can help you stay ahead of emerging roles and global opportunities.

Some helpful starting points:

- Adam Elman – Frequently shares sustainability and climate-related job opportunities across industries and regions.

- Lois Freeke – Actively highlights international roles and market shifts, particularly across global sustainability and ESG career spaces.
- Erin McGoff - Advice with Erin offers expert insights and practical tips to help you navigate life's career challenges with confidence.

Adam and Lois are both consistently active on LinkedIn, sharing job alerts, career advice and opportunities that many people may not otherwise come across. AdvicewithErin is less 'climate' focused, but offers real, practical advice in navigating career conversations and decisions, which are often muddled with complex and misleading questions.

As briefly mentioned in Part 2, I'd recommend job boards such as Do Good Jobs (Work with Purpose | Mahi ki te Kaupapa) in Aotearoa New Zealand. Another would be Probably Good, which is a nonprofit organisation dedicated to helping people build careers that are good for them and good for the world. Search online, and you will undoubtedly find other organisations in your country/ region that are signposting similar opportunities. And if there isn't? Maybe that's the opening for you: recruiters have great potential to shape and influence the future of work (as we've seen with Amy's story). If Do Good Jobs (or the equivalent) doesn't exist where you live, maybe you could be the one to fill that gap?

Others do this too, and depending on your location, sector or style of work, different people will resonate with you. I recommend spending time curating your own feed: search terms like "sustainability" or "climate careers", follow people whose advice feels relevant, and gradually build a network that supports your aspirations. Think of these names simply as good starting points if you're not sure where to begin.

Reading

Some of these books I read years ago. Others are currently open on my desk as I write this. All of them, in one way or another, have shaped how I think about climate, work, systems, and responsibility. Some have directly influenced the pages you've just read. Others have done their work more quietly, threading themselves into how I show up in this space.

Please don't feel any pressure to read every book listed here to "do climate right." Take what serves you. Read one or many. Pick up a hardback, borrow a paperback, listen to an audiobook on your commute, or download an e-book if that's your style. What matters most is not the format or the volume, but that you engage in a way that works for you.

Your learning journey won't look like mine, and it doesn't need to. The point isn't to read everything. The point is to begin.

I'm certain I've missed some brilliant books. This list isn't definitive. It's simply a starting point. If it introduces you to even one new idea, voice, or perspective that stays with you, then it's done its job.

- *50 Things You Need to Know About Heat Pumps — Graham Hendra*
- *A Bigger Picture — Vanessa Nakate*
- *Abundance — Ezra Klein & Derek Thompson*

- *All We Can Save — ed. Ayana Elizabeth Johnson & Katharine K. Wilkinson*
- *Aroha — Dr Hinemoa Elder*
- *Awesome Earth – Joan Bransfield Graham*
- *Brief Answers to Big Questions — Stephen Hawking*
- *Carbon Capture — Howard J. Herzog*
- *Chief Sustainability Officers at Work — Chrissa Pagitsas*
- *Climate Change Is Racist — Jeremy Williams*
- *Climate Justice — Mary Robinson*
- *Designed to Perform — Tom Dollard*
- *Doughnut Economics — Kate Raworth*
- *Five Times Faster — Simon Sharpe*
- *Higher Ground — Alison Taylor*
- *Hot Mess — Matt Winning*
- *How Bad Are Bananas? — Mike Berners-Lee*
- *How to Avoid a Climate Disaster — Bill Gates*
- *Invisible Women – Caroline Criado-Perez*
- *Leave Only Footprints – Conor Knighton*
- *Let My People Go Surfing — Yvon Chouinard*
- *Material World — Ed Conway*
- *Moral Ambition — Rutger Bregman*
- *Net Positive — Paul Polman & Andrew Winston*
- *Nga Kupu Wero — ed. Witi Ihimaera*
- *No Miracles Needed — Mark Z. Jacobson*
- *Not the End of the World — Hannah Ritchie*
- *Positive Tipping Points – Tim Lenton*
- *Project Drawdown — Paul Hawken*
- *Regenesis — George Monbiot*
- *Sapiens — Yuval Noah Harari*
- *Speed & Scale — John Doerr*

- *The Carbon Almanac — Multiple contributors*
- *The Climate Book — Greta Thunberg*
- *The Climate Mindset Manifesto — Katelyn Prendiville*
- *The Forgotten Forest — Robert Venell*
- *The Future of Energy (series) — John Armstrong*
- *The Future We Choose — Christiana Figueres & Tom Rivett-Carnac*
- *The Intersectional Environmentalist — Leah Thomas*
- *The Overstory — Richard Powers*
- *The Rise & Fall of the Dinosaurs — Steve Brusatte*
- *The Serviceberry – John Burgoyne*
- *The Trading Game: A Confession — Gary Stevenson*
- *The Uninhabitable Earth — David Wallace-Wells*
- *The West Texas Power Plant That Saved the World — Andy Bowman*
- *This Changes Everything — Naomi Klein*
- *Trade Wars are Class Wars – Matthew C. Klein*
- *Urbanism for a Difficult Future — Korkut Onaran*
- *Vulture Capitalism — Grace Blakeley*
- *We Are the Weather — Jonathan Safran Foer*

Podcasts

- *Watt Matters* — FORESIGHT Media Group
  Explores the evolving energy system and pathways to decarbonisation.
- *The Climate Question* — BBC World Service
  Global perspectives on climate challenges and solutions.
- *My Climate Journey* — Jason Jacobs, Cody Simms & Yin Lu
  Interviews with founders, investors and practitioners working on climate tech and action.
- *Just to Save the World* — hosted by Phil the Fixer
  Grassroots activism and real-world stories of climate action.
- *The Big Green Money Show* — BBC Radio 5 with Deborah Meaden
  Where finance meets the environment — how business choices impact climate.
- *Heated* — Limina House
  Connecting the dots between climate, health (including pandemics), and politics.
- *TED Climate + Climate Curious* — TED and TEDxLondon
  Encourages curiosity-led conversations to make climate action more accessible.
- *Sustainability Uncovered* — edie.net
  Business-focused sustainability insights and interviews.
- *Climate Rising* — Harvard Business School
  Discusses corporate climate strategy, innovation and leadership.

- *The Climate Business* — Vincent Heeringa (NZ)
  New Zealand-based perspectives on business and sustainability.
- *Net Zero: The Road to 2050* — Newsroom
  A look into energy transition, infrastructure and policy decisions shaping NZ's decarbonisation.
- *Zero Ambitions* — hosted by Jeff, Dan & Alex
  Exploring decarbonisation of the built environment and modern building practices.
- *Accelerate to Zero* — BE-ST
  Innovation and industry transformation towards net zero in construction.
- *BetaTALK* — Nathan Gamblin (BetaTeach)
  Honest conversations with heating engineers and industry professionals.
- *ZERO Carbon Construction* — ZERO Construct
  Highlights the shift to low-carbon building techniques and tools.
- *The Home Energy Show* — Heatio
  Practical energy efficiency advice for homeowners and installers.
- On My Mind — *UNICEF*
  Real conversations about youth mental health, resilience and coping strategies.
- The Happiness Lab — *Dr Laurie Santos (Yale)*
  Science-backed tools for happiness and wellbeing — perfect for reframing mindset during high-pressure advocacy or leadership challenges.

Acknowledgements

This book has taken over two years to write. But it is really the product of far more than that: years of conversations, emails, meetings, seminars, coffee catch-ups, ideas that strike late at night when staring at the ceiling, and many laughs over a Guinness or two. Every chapter carries bits of the people and moments that have shaped those years. So I would firstly like to thank you, the reader, for picking up this book and coming on this journey with me.

If this book ends up being truly successful, then, at least in theory, I may be writing myself out of a job. We don't actually need a world full of sustainability managers. Similar to Anje's point about not needing a world of vegans. We need workplaces where everyone understands their impact, takes responsibility, and makes more conscious decisions. I once heard a sustainability manager at a conference in London say she hoped her role would one day become redundant. Just as most companies no longer rely on dedicated safety officers because health and safety are embedded in everyday practice, sustainability should become a standard, not a speciality.

With that in mind, here's to everyone who helped me towards an early retirement (or redundancy).

My deepest thanks go to everyone who generously took the time to be interviewed for this book. Your openness, honesty, and willingness to give me your time, share your stories, doubts, and lessons form the backbone of these pages. This book quite simply would not exist without you. I'm grateful not only for your insights but also for the time you carved out for me. I left the interviews until quite late in my writing process because I wanted something a bit more concrete to talk about with each of you. Your feedback, engagement, and support have meant so much and really helped me get this book across the line.

Thank you to my colleagues, clients, collaborators, and peers, past and present. I had no idea that a placement year working for a small building services consultancy would open the door to such a wide range of buildings, projects, and conversations. Above all, it introduced me to brilliant, kind, thoughtful and occasionally sarcastic people who have shaped how I think about work and impact. To those I've shared ideas with, challenged assumptions alongside, learned from, and occasionally moaned to, this book is richer because of those conversations.

Thank you to my family and friends for your encouragement, perspective, and patience, and for tolerating far more climate-related conversation than anyone should reasonably be expected to endure. You've grounded me when I've drifted too far into the abstract and reminded me that this work is about real people and real lives.

I also want to acknowledge the mentors and role models who have shaped my thinking over the last decade and more. Some have been managers and directors. Some have been colleagues in different teams. Some have been clients or partners. Some I've never met in person, but have learned from through conversations, articles, and the strange but powerful world of LinkedIn.

There are two individuals I really want to take a moment to mention.

The first is my sister. Abigail, I've always looked up to you. You are driven, intelligent, hard-working, passionate, and just generally a lovely person to be around. I feel so proud to be your brother. Watching you shape your career in recent years, align your skillset with your personality, and step into your strengths has been inspiring. You deserve every success that comes your way. You are one of the biggest inspirations behind this book. Thank you for everything. And from the other side of the world, through these pages, I miss you.

The second is Emma. When I first started my career, you took me out on one of my first days and taught me the ropes. But from that day on, you went far beyond what was required. Many people have guided and supported me over the years, but you helped me build confidence, too. You have always stood firmly by your values and shown me that work can, and should, align with positive social outcomes. That we can choose to use our roles to support others and strengthen community. Thank you for your steady encouragement and shining example.

Dear Jude. Thank you for putting up with my monotone voice talking about air conditioning and heat pumps for the last ten years. You've stood beside me, challenged me when I needed it, backed me when I've doubted myself, and supported me in more ways than I could ever list. You are the reason we moved to the other side of the world. You pushed me out of my comfort zone, and I am endlessly grateful that you did.

You are brave, fiercely intelligent, funny, and kind beyond words. I've learned more from you than you probably realise.

You've listened to half-formed ideas, endured countless monologues, sat through presentation run-throughs, read drafts long before they were ready, and supported me through every stage of this process. This book is better because of you. I am better because of you. I'm incredibly grateful for the life we've built together, and for everything still to come as we grow old and grey (older and greyer).

Lastly, Marley. Our little cocker spaniel has brought more happiness into my life than she will ever understand. Sitting at my laptop late into the night, with you curled up next to me, snoring without a care in the world, has been one of the quiet joys of writing this book. Life can be stressful and complicated, but watching a small animal wander around your home, safe and fully part of the family, puts things back into perspective. You've influenced this work more than you'll ever know, not least because you can't read.

To everyone who has supported me, engaged in meandering conversations, sparked an idea, challenged my thinking, or shared a moment of frustration or hope, I am immensely grateful for you and your time.

Thank you.

FIRST PUBLISHED 2026

BY STARTING WHERE YOU ARE PRESS

AOTEAROA NEW ZEALAND

ISBN 978-1-0671327-0-5 (PAPERBACK)

ISBN 978-1-0671327-1-2 (EBOOK)

NEW ZEALAND

ISBN 978-1-0671327-0-5 (PAPERBACK)
ISBN 978-1-0671327-1-2 (EBOOK)

COPYRIGHT © 2026 RYAN PHILP

FIRST PUBLISHED 2026

BY STARTING WHERE YOU ARE PRESS

www.ingramcontent.com/pod-product-compliance
Lightning Source LLC
Chambersburg PA
CBHW070411290526
45791CB00005B/1702